WATCHMEN...
OR
WOLVES?

CHRIS AND MICHELE NEAL

WATCHMEN... OR WOLVES?

DEMONIC TAKEOVER IN THE HOUSE OF GOD

FOREWORD BY
THE RIGHT REVEREND DR GAVIN ASHENDEN
Former Chaplain to Her Majesty the Queen

Watchmen... or Wolves? Demonic Takeover in the House of God

Graphic design and typesetting by JWC Creative. www.jwccreative.com

ISBN: 9781671453661

FOREWORD

I am delighted to be able to commend this important book. We are reminded that "Where there is no vision the people perish." Proverbs 29:18 in the King James translation offers a stark warning. The ESV gets us closer to the spirit of the original by translating it "Where there is no prophetic vision the people cast off restraint but blessed is he who keeps the law."

This book rekindles the prophetic vision of what the Church is called to be and what the principles of the Kingdom are as we find them set out in the revelation of Scripture. The people we live amongst have cast off restraint, and a large part of the Church has behaved like an over-indulgent tipsy child-minder and patted them on the head and hoped that they have a good time.

Yet we face two alarming and related experiences. The first is the obvious assault on the Judaeo-Christian moral tradition by a re-invigorated utopian Left, in combination with the fundamentalist rationalism or a materialist scientism. Unable to face the question 'why something is there rather than nothing', the scientific materialists settle for an assault on a spiritual instinct they are tone deaf to, and are unable to replace the profound moral virtues of Christianity with anything other than the pleasure principle. The new Left are doing what they did a century ago, and hysterically attacking both the Christian family and the Christian Church in order to replace the Father Creator with the State and human pride. The other experience is the alarming sense that in so many places, the presence of God has withdrawn from the Church.

Chris and Michele Neal write chillingly; "*We have walked*

into churches where you can tangibly feel the presence of the Lord. We have also walked into churches that once felt alive but now feel dead, and a cold shiver has come over us." I remember when I first experienced this contrast in a dramatic and direct way myself. I had spent 7 years praying daily with fellow clergy in a Church I was associated with in South London, and had been very grateful for a sense of God's presence I rather took for granted. I should not have done. Returning for the funeral of one of those colleagues twenty years later I walked into the Church and almost gasped. The sense of empty chill was palpable. To begin with, I looked for furnishing that I thought must have been stripped away to explain the dull grey atmosphere. But looking around I could see nothing physical had changed. What had changed was the absence of God's presence. Precisely what kind of corruption drives away the Holy Spirit is a matter for God Himself. He is always inviting us to repent and is very patient with us. But hardened hearts and obtuse minds allow Him no access, and there comes a point where He is driven away and removes Himself. I knew that the last Rector of the Parish had been a vocal LGBT campaigner and found myself wondering if that was the final straw for the Holy Spirit?

It seems that an increasing number of the clergy have capitulated to the spirit of the age and adopted a relativistic sense of moral and spiritual values. There is little doubt that the phenomenon of the ordination of women has contributed to this. Raised on an unremitting diet of uncritiqued feminism, two generations of women have become conditioned to egalitarian and relativistic principles that provide a political worldview rather than a Christian one. Equality is a concept that lends itself more easily to numbers than to values, and when attached to values, often functions as a trojan horse that sets out to undermine or displace Judaeo-Christian culture.

Despite the clarity and witness of Scripture and the constant murmur of prophetic warning we have known over the decades, the sense that God's withdrawal from a Church that teaches the opposite of the purity of heart that Jesus places so centrally in His teaching, is becoming more widespread.

The Church faces an ideological assault on sexual and moral purity from an un-boundaried LGBT+ culture that places the romantic and the erotic at the centre of the human quest. St Paul warns that a society given over to idolatry will experience ever greater levels of distorted sexuality and sexual identity. Instead of calling the Church and society away from the idolatries that distract from the living God, so many of the clergy treat what the Bible calls sin as an aspect of the so-called human right to self-expression and pleasure, and under the cover of the notion of 'inclusion', encourage and promote it.

Jesus warned that so far from promoting inclusion, He had come to warn against a permanent exclusion from the Kingdom and call people to repentance. This central aspect of His teaching is not only ignored but silenced as a relativistic universalism is imposed on the Gospel narrative.

The Church also faces an assault from an uncompromising Islam that moves inexorably forward propelled both by demographics and by the free pass that progressive clergy and public commentators give it. They entirely misunderstand that Islam is uncompromising in its assault on the integrity of the Gospels and so on the claims of Jesus Himself.

The Church in the West is at the most critical moment in its history for the last 500 years. Voices like those of Chris and Michele Neal are badly needed if the prophetic call to repent is to be heard. We are invited to identify and resist the corruption of what St John theologically identified as 'the world', which continues its assault on the integrity of the Church and its faithfulness to Jesus. We are reminded that the gates of hell will not prevail.

Maranatha, Lord Jesus.

The Right Reverend Dr Gavin Ashenden
SSC, LLB, BA, MTh, Ph.D.

Missionary Bishop for the Christian Episcopal Church

ENDORSEMENTS

'Chris and Michele Neal's latest offering to the people of God is a *no excuses* course for our times that clearly states where and how the Church is operating in compromise and without the necessary fear of God that, when in place, is meant to be the counterculture to what is commonly accepted amongst modern-day Christians. If you have never understood the difference between a watchman or a wolf, this book defines what they each are and provides Scriptural references for what God has already told us about them in His Word. This is a *must-read* for every church leader!'

The Reverend Charlynne M. Boddie; Minister, International Speaker, and Author of '*No Appointments Necessary*' and '*True Grid*'. charlynne.com

'The title of Chris and Michele Neal's new book, '*Watchmen ... or Wolves?*' illustrates the disturbing trend within churches today to conform to the world, ignore the Truth of God's Word and deceive those attending these churches. This excellent book leaves no stone unturned. It is both disturbing and challenging. Thoroughly researched, backed up with powerful Scripture references and providing plenty of up-to-date examples, this book exposes the incredible assault on the Truth of God's Word and on those who would uphold the Truth. And, as the title implies, the assault is coming from within the Church; 'Watchmen' who are in reality Wolves in Sheep's clothing! Whilst many in the Church are falling prey to the deceptive schemes of the Enemy and unbiblical thinking, this book can be counted among the top clear voices sounding a clear warning AND call to action for those willing to heed. This book will play a profound role in helping the reader discern God's Truth and will be a valuable resource in this post-modern culture.'

Day Ashton; Author of *'Moments of Encouragement'*. Freelance Writer and Bible Teacher. Blogger for 'Day's Meditations' – daysmeditations.wordpress.com and In 'Defence of the Truth' – dayashtonuk.wixsite.com/indefenceofthetruth

'A timely wake-up call to a Church gone adrift from its Biblical moorings.'

The Reverend Melvin Tinker, Senior Minister St Johns Newland, Hull. Author of *'That Hideous Strength: How The West was Lost'*.

'In these days, perhaps the greatest need for those who seek to stand faithfully for the gospel of Jesus Christ, is not just to see things clearly but to take action in line with this sight. We cannot approach an essentially spiritual problem by all too human pragmatic or political means. We know this from scripture. Rather, by the light of the Bible, the sword of the Spirit, we can see and act in the Holy Spirit's grace and truth, like our Lord. Our struggle is not against flesh and blood and so our response must be likewise spiritual, full of grace and truth. Chris and Michele Neal have done us a great service in gathering the relevant scriptures together, in helping us to see their contemporary application and so equipping us to take a stand. It may not be comfortable reading, but for every faithful disciple it will refresh our sight and make us all the more dependent on the only one who was, and is, full of grace and truth.'

The Reverend John Parker

'This book is like a Braveheart trumpet call to the church in our generation. It's written with a caring heart for the souls that Christ purchased with His own blood. Written with boldness addressing the issues, but with longing to see the Church be the free Bride that Christ will return for. I congratulate Chris and Michele on this excellent book.'

Francois Botes; Prophetic and Music Ministry. www.francoisbotes.org

'This is a timely book, helping us all to get back to the foundations of what we believe. It is a book to re-read frequently, and its length and straightforward style will help many who are struggling with the current issues the authors clearly address. In the name of Jesus our Saviour and Lord, I thank you both for your labours and faith and courage.'

The Reverend Canon Stuart Holt B.Ed.

'Sizzling tough love with brave energy, identifying and classifying the most up to date areas of abandonment and departure infiltrating the Church, with scriptural warnings. Deceptive times, watch and pray.'

Patricia C. McGlennon, Author of '*Last Call for the Church*'

The following endorsement is from a retired church leader, and out of respect for their request for anonymity, we have agreed not to publish this person's name:

'In this hard-hitting and uncompromising book, the authors uncover how secular humanism is infiltrating the Church and poisoning her from within. Faithful Christians must be alert to the issues raised and insist their leaders value and teach God's truth in all its fullness. I hope the warnings in this book will be heeded by all who love the Lord.'

Anon

'The chief danger that confronts the coming century will be religion without the Holy Ghost, Christianity without Christ, forgiveness without repentance, salvation without regeneration, politics without God, heaven without hell.' – The chillingly prophetic words of General William Booth (1829 - 1912), English Methodist preacher and founder of The Salvation Army.

DEDICATION

We dedicate this book to our beloved fathers, Cyril Neal and David Cooper, who have passed away and are now in the presence of the Lord. We miss you both so very much.

This work is ultimately dedicated to the glory of God. Without our faith in His Son Jesus Christ as our Lord and Saviour, and all that He has taught us in our journey with Him for over a quarter of a century, this book would never have been written.

ACKNOWLEDGEMENTS

It is with our deepest gratitude that we offer our thanks to The Right Reverend Dr Gavin Ashenden for undertaking the task of reading the manuscript and writing the Foreword for this book, all whilst juggling a very busy life in many aspects of Church, radio, TV and social media in his personal effort to alert followers of Christ to the dire mess the Church has got itself into.

We wish to also extend our thanks to all those who have written endorsements for this book; The Reverend Charlynne Boddie, The Reverend Melvin Tinker, The Reverend John Parker, The Reverend Canon Stuart Holt, Francois Botes, Day Ashton, Patricia McGlennon, and finally a retired minister who wishes to remain anonymous. We appreciate greatly the time you have all taken out of your own busy schedules to read the manuscript and write words in support of this work.

Knowing that we are not alone in our thinking, and that a significant number within the Church are awake and alert to what is going on in these times, is a great encouragement to us. The work is hard, but your companionship in this undertaking helps to lighten the load and bolster us up to face the battle.

Thank you to Jason Carter at JWC Creative for using your God-given gift in getting this book published. Neither Michele nor I possess the ability to turn a manuscript document on our computer into a published book! Thank you so much Jason.

Finally, we would like to thank the handful of like-minded brothers and sisters in Christ whom the Lord has brought into our lives since 2011 – the year when God decided to wake us up out of our spiritual slumber. Your encouragement and support with regards to this book, and all the previous books we have written, has kept us anchored to fulfilling what the Lord is compelling us to do.

God bless each and every person who has been involved in this book. Your fellowship with us on this journey means a lot to us.

CONTENTS

INTRODUCTION

The Reason for this Book

"Beware of the false prophets, [teachers] who come to you dressed as sheep [appearing gentle and innocent], but inwardly are ravenous wolves." – Matthew 7:15 AMP

The journey that has culminated in the writing of this book began in 2008. At that time, we lived in Lincolnshire and were members of a church there. Michele has always been a fairly shy person, never wanting to put herself in a position of going to the front to say anything. Due to certain health difficulties, she is able to spend quite a bit of time each day shutting herself away in a quiet space to pray, listening to what the Lord may want to say to her personally about her own life in Christ and areas that He may want her to work on. She also remains alert to anything the Holy Spirit may reveal about wider Church issues.

On one particular day, she felt the Lord overwhelm her with a word to give to the church we attended. The thought of standing up to speak something in front of a group of people absolutely terrified her, but she knew she had to write down what God was speaking to her. She realised that it was a word of prophecy and that He wanted her to read it out in a church meeting. Having never experienced the Lord giving her a word of prophecy for any church before, she knew that she had to obey Him, but she was naturally very anxious about doing it. What would people think?!

For the entire week it pressed heavily on her mind, but despite her immense anxiety, we attended the next meeting. It was a special midweek gathering where all were encouraged to seek more of the Holy Spirit, and give words of knowledge or prophecy if anyone felt the Lord was laying something on their hearts. This seemed a good environment for Michele to speak out what the Lord had given to her, since the leaders were encouraging people to operate in the gifts of the Spirit. Out of respect, she first decided to give the word to the ministry team before the meeting started and asked them if they would kindly give it a quick read to 'test' that it was of the Lord. Michele knew it was from the Lord, but she wanted to present it to the leaders beforehand for reassurance.

She sat down and waited. After about ten minutes, the team called me over to see them. They politely informed me that they believed the word Michele wanted to give was 'too weighty' and that it 'needed the rough edges knocking off'. I was stunned by this response. I had read the word that the Lord had given to her, and it was a powerful, encouraging message exhorting believers to rise up against any spirit of fear, to resist the arrows of deception that Satan hurls at us, and to stand on the Word of God in the daily battles that we face against the kingdom of darkness. This clearly lined up with the Words of Scripture.

I then went over to Michele and, as gently as I could, I told her that the team would not allow her to give the message to the church. I watched my wife visibly shake from head to foot at being prevented from speaking out something the Lord had instructed her to do. Somehow, she felt the Lord tell her to sit there in the meeting and not run out of the door. She felt that He wanted her to sit quietly and witness for herself what happens when those who are appointed as His watchmen over the flock believe they can control the work of the Holy Spirit in the lives of other believers; stifling His powerful words for the sake of not wanting to make anyone feel uncomfortable with words that they consider 'too weighty'.

Michele found that, no matter how hard she tried, she could not enter into worship in the meeting at all. She felt that a darkness had descended into the midst of the meeting, and that she was watching something taking place in some sort of open vision which the Lord wanted her to see. This troubled her greatly.

When we got home that night, she hardly slept at all. She cried for hours, pouring out her heart to the Lord, feeling that she had failed Him by not speaking the message and not having the courage to challenge the team leaders about their personal opinion and their rejection of her giving the message. The next morning Michele shut herself off in her prayer room for a very long time. Again, she poured out her soul to the Lord about this distressing incident. She said to Him, "Lord, what was **that** about? Why did you give me that message to speak to the church which they then prevented me from speaking in the meeting? You knew how afraid I was of standing up to speak, but I overcame my fear and was willing to obey you. But they rejected your message and would not let me deliver it. My heart is broken because I feel like I have failed you."

Suddenly, the Holy Spirit invaded her soul with words that catapulted her from the pit of despair to a place of abundant joy within a split second! He spoke to her in direct answer to her heartbroken prayer. He said, "My child, you have not failed Me. What you experienced was a very painful test. I wanted to see if you would rise above your fears and be willing to obey My instructions to you to stand before the people to speak a message out loud. It does not matter that you were prevented from speaking it; what I was looking for in you was your obedience to Me and your willingness to do what in your natural self is the last thing that you would ever want to do. Well done My child! You passed the test that I took you through, and I know that I can trust you to deliver any words I give you in the future, in whichever way I choose for you to do it."

Michele came rushing out of her prayer room with tears streaming down her face with sheer joy! I have never seen my wife so overcome with so many emotions all at once! She did not know what to do with all the joy that was racing around inside of her! She ran around the house shouting at the top of her voice with thanksgiving and praise to God!

This incident has never left our minds. It was the spark that ignited the flame of all the Lord has taken Michele through, using her to write her books since 2011, all of which are a 'Wake Up' call to the Church. Her whole mindset now is, "If the Church won't let me speak out loud what the Lord is wanting to say, then I will write it all in books. God has told me to deliver His messages, and that is what I will do…silently but powerfully…in books."

The book you are holding in your hands is Michele's fifth book, which I am co-authoring with her, as it is a message that is a great burden in both of our hearts. It contains many of God's 'weighty Words' and 'rough edges' that the Church would prefer not to hear. From Genesis to Revelation, Holy Scripture is full of God's weighty Words, and God has not deemed it necessary to shave off the rough edges just to make things more comfortable for us to hear.

It is our heart's desire that by the end of this book, **all** who profess to be followers of Christ would be so troubled by the state of what is happening in the Church today, that with God's help, they will want to search their hearts deeply, and do whatever is necessary to get to the place where they can sincerely declare the following powerful verse of Scripture to be a truthful fact in relation to their own personal life in Christ:

*"**We have renounced disgraceful ways** (secret thoughts, feelings, desires and underhandedness, the methods and arts that men hide through shame); **we refuse to deal craftily** (to practice trickery and cunning) **or to adulterate or handle dishonestly the Word of God, but we state the truth openly (clearly and candidly).**"* – 2 Corinthians 4:2 AMPC (Authors' emphasis)

This verse is one which is action-orientated, causing us to not be able to escape from its pointed instruction. It demands our attention, showing us that we need to ask ourselves the deeply probing questions that the verse brings out into the open:

a) **Have I renounced disgraceful ways** – the secret thoughts, feelings, desires and underhandedness, the methods and arts that men hide through shame?

b) **Do I refuse to deal craftily** – to practice trickery and cunning, or to adulterate or handle dishonestly the Word of God?

c) **Do I state the truth openly** – clearly and candidly?

So, with all this in mind, we will now begin to share with you what the Lord has been revealing to us over recent years. It is our deepest prayer that God will do a mighty waking up of His Church, bringing it to repentance before Jesus returns…

God's Watchmen

In the Bible, God's watchmen were those whom He called to shepherd His people, teaching them in the ways of His Word, and to keep watch over them in order to protect them from approaching enemy attacks. More importantly, His shepherds were required to warn the people not to succumb to the ways, the beliefs and the cultural climate of the nations around them. Their role was also to warn the people of God's judgement if they were going astray or were in outright rebellion. His watchmen were to sound the alarm, but if the people failed to respond to their warning, then whatever consequence befell them, it was their own responsibility, not the watchman's (see Ezekiel 33:1-5).

Throughout this book, we mostly use the word 'shepherd' in relation to those in positions of leadership and authority in the Church who are ultimately responsible for the care of the flock, but with the full understanding that the biblical sense of this word is that of a **watchman** for the Lord.

We have sub-titled this book 'Demonic Takeover in the House of God'.

The Cambridge Dictionary (www.dictionary.cambridge.org) defines the word 'Takeover' as follows:

1. To begin to have control of something.
2. To replace someone or something.

The general Google definition of this word is:

1. An act of assuming control of something.

When something or someone comes along to 'begin to have control' of a situation, it means that the original thing has become weak. When control is assumed by another party, this can be for the good…but it can also be for evil.

In recent years we have noticed that something strange has come upon the Church which ought to stand out like a blazing warning light. This 'something' has caused leaders in the Church to begin twisting the Word of God in order to accommodate the culture that is enveloping it; like a snake slithering along, creeping up unknowingly on its prey, and then swallowing it whole.

Up until recently, all appeared relatively well within the Church, with its ability to remain strong in the face of those who oppose God's teachings. But somewhere along the way, those in high positions in the Church seem to have stopped keeping a biblical watch over their flock. It now appears that God's watchmen have either grown tired of upholding and preaching obedience to His Word, or they purposefully intend to preach a 'new gospel'. Many people who claim to be Christians, do not like hearing sound, convicting, biblical truth anymore because it makes them feel uncomfortable, and some even take great offense. What now seems to be heard from the pulpits is that God has 'got it wrong' and the Church feels obliged to correct His 'mistakes'! We may not hear those actual words from leaders, but the inference is there in the type of things that are now being preached; subtle heretical teaching that implies a new 'understanding' that God's Word is 'fluid' and can be open to all kinds of interpretation, enabling it to fit comfortably with the agendas of those in the Church who want to remain as they are, rather than be delivered from their sins and transformed by the power of the Holy Spirit. The Church is increasingly buying into the ways of the culture and society of our time, and the following proverb sums it up well:

"Like a muddied spring or a polluted well are the righteous who give way to the wicked." – Proverbs 25:26 NIV

This sudden change in the attitude, thinking and beliefs of those in positions of authority in the Church is nothing short of rebellion against the anointed role that God has placed upon them as His watchmen. Embracing the ideologies and practices of the surrounding secular culture, affirming anything and everything in the name of 'acceptance and tolerance' is not what God has called them to do. God's shepherds are no longer keeping watch over their flock, and this is a very dangerous position for the **flock** to be in.

This alarming about-turn in the way the Church is heading should be a wake-up call to all who profess to be followers of Christ. Faithful and obedient Christians should be fleeing from these false shepherds like a flock of sheep scattering for their lives at the frenzied advance of a pack of ravenous wolves! Many church leaders, who we once held in high regard as faithful shepherds, are now beginning to unmask their real identity. Underneath their 'sheep's clothing' which they proudly wear in their role as God's shepherd, they are being persuaded by those in high office above them that they must put aside what God says and instead listen to and accept 'new teachings' that are nothing short of heresy. This has resulted in them inwardly turning into preachers of lies, false teachers (wolves), and tragically, the sheep in their congregations are their unsuspecting prey.

Whilst still appearing, outwardly, to be our faithful shepherds, and still supposedly keeping watch over their flock, somewhere in the 'hallowed' halls of Church hierarchy, where the sheep rarely venture, pernicious seeds of subtle deception have been sown into the minds of our shepherds and have taken root. As we saw above, the Cambridge dictionary definition of the word 'Takeover' included 'to replace someone or something'. Our church shepherds have allowed Satan's deception to replace biblical truth. Not aware of the deception that is taking place in these secret ecclesiastical chambers, or the effect that it is having upon their own souls, Satan has managed to ensnare those at the very top of religious circles with his original 'Garden of Eden' lie; "Did God **really** say…?" (see Genesis 3:1).

Once Satan has managed to persuade Church hierarchy to question God's Word, he knows that these people will be able to influence those who are under their authority, creating ways that will cause them to believe that the long-held beliefs and doctrines of authentic Christianity are now 'an injustice against people's human rights' to live however they want. Satan will convince leaders that the Church needs to apologise to the world for preaching to them Jesus' Gospel message of salvation – the message that, in order to be saved, we must confess and repent of our sins, put our faith in Jesus Christ, and be born again by the Holy Spirit, which will result in a complete transformation in us, from craving the things of sin to hungering and thirsting for the things that please God.

Having duly convinced leaders that these foundations of Christianity are an 'obstacle' to Church growth, Satan will then persuade them that the Church needs to redefine itself, reinvent itself and relabel itself as a 'new model' of Christianity, with its whole focus on 'love and affirmation' as being the ultimate 'salvation solution' to the ills and the evils of this world. This deception then mutates into a 'declaration of freedom', claiming that there is no need for confession and repentance anymore; that these biblical requirements are an ancient and outdated millstone around everyone's necks that they could thoroughly do without!

This 'new Christianity' is being rapidly rolled out across the world at an **inexorable** rate. It is bringing people into the Church in their thousands. Welcoming people in as they are and letting them remain as they are in their sin, this new and modern version of 'Church' sounds like the sort of place that most people would love to belong to; after all, most people do not like to be told that there is something wrong with them that needs repenting of and changing! But in Romans 4:3(a) KJ21, the apostle Paul said, *"What saith the Scripture?"* Rather than wanting to diligently know what the Scriptures say about what God requires us to do to live as faithful, obedient Christians, the Church wants to carve out its own version of Christianity, taking on new ventures and projects that allows sin to have a comfortable seat in the House of God. What the Scriptures have to say seems to be the furthest thing from their minds, or at the very least, having read the Scriptures, there is now an attitude of, "Oh, we will find a way around that somehow."

But the issue before us is that the Church that Jesus Christ established is based on sinners being convicted of their sinfulness by the power of the Holy Spirit, being brought to a place of confession and repentance of their sin, being transformed by the Holy Spirit, and then living lives of obedience to His Word. Bygone generations would have had no doubt what it meant to be a Christian. But what we see happening in the Church today is far removed from what our Christian forefathers poured their lives out for. Casting aside obedience to God's Word to please the unrepentant is not something that the Church should be proudly boasting about.

Much of the Church is now a simmering cauldron of confusion. The increasing lies being portrayed as 'new Christian teaching' have been creeping bit by bit into the minds of rising numbers of our local church leaders, driven by the agendas and the stealth of those who have appointed them. Some brave leaders have had the courage to challenge the hierarchy, but most seem to be 'toeing the line' for the sake of a life of an outward appearance of unity and stability. But the lid can only be kept on the pot for so long. At some point, the pressure will build to such an extent that the contents of the cauldron will explode, leaving a stinking mess.

This book is our combined effort to sound the alarm bells as loud as we possibly can, to wake up and warn believers of what is happening right under their noses. This book is about the demonic takeover that is happening in the Church, right from the very top, and is filtering its way down to us ordinary folk. Satan's nice-sounding lies have weakened our leaders, they have fallen for the temptation to compromise with the ways of the world, and Satan has slithered in with the intent of **taking over** our complacent, compromising, wavering situation. Now that he has infiltrated the Church at the highest levels, we sheep in the pews cannot sit by hoping that Satan and his demons will just get bored and decide to leave in a nice orderly fashion! Wake up! The enemy is in the camp, and his plan is to **destroy** the sheep, **not** join them in worshipping the One who they profess is their Saviour!

The Church needs to get back to the mindset of "What saith the Scripture?" We need to be like the Berean believers who daily sought the Scriptures for themselves to check that what they were hearing Paul teach them was true (see Acts 17:11). If we abandon all that we have known to be true of God's Word, and decide to agree with, go along with, or merely tolerate deceptive teaching (Satan's lies) for the sake of not rocking the boat, we could face spiritual disaster:

"...keeping your faith [leaning completely on God with absolute trust and confidence in His guidance] and having a good conscience; ***for some [people] have rejected [their moral compass] and have made a shipwreck of their faith."*** – 1 Timothy 1:19 AMP (Authors' emphasis)

So as not to be misunderstood, we want to say right from the start that we acknowledge the many good and faithful servants who work tirelessly to proclaim the true Gospel message, teach the Scriptures without error and firmly hold to the importance of confession and repentance of sin. The purpose of this book is to expose, to those who sit in the pews, the truth that in some Church denominations a subtle but wholesale slide into apostasy is gathering momentum at an ever-increasing pace. This book is also a plea that those behind this deception will repent publicly, seek God's forgiveness, and return to obedience to His Word.

So, without further ado, let's now begin by looking at what the role of God's shepherds **should** be.

Chapter 1

THE ROLE OF GOD'S SHEPHERDS

"Therefore, I strongly urge the elders among you [pastors, spiritual leaders of the church], as a fellow elder and as an eyewitness [called to testify] of the sufferings of Christ, as well as one who shares in the glory that is to be revealed: shepherd and guide and protect the flock of God among you, exercising oversight not under compulsion, but voluntarily, according to the will of God; and not [motivated] for shameful gain, but with wholehearted enthusiasm; not lording it over those assigned to your care [do not be arrogant or overbearing], but be examples [of Christian living] to the flock [set a pattern of integrity for your congregation]." - 1 Peter 5:1-3 AMP

"So guard yourselves and God's people. Feed and shepherd God's flock — his church, purchased with his own blood—over which the Holy Spirit has appointed you as leaders... Remember the three years I was with you —my constant watch and care over you night and day, and my many tears for you." - Acts 20:28, 31

Let's begin by taking a brief look at some earthly shepherds; those who were keeping watch over their flock on the night that Jesus Christ was born:

"In the same region there were shepherds staying out in the fields, keeping watch over their flock by night. And an angel of the Lord suddenly stood before them, and the glory of the Lord flashed and

shone around them, and they were terribly frightened. But the angel said to them, "Do not be afraid; for behold, I bring you good news of great joy which will be for all the people. For this day in the city of David there has been born for you a Savior, who is Christ the Lord (the Messiah)." – Luke 2:8-11 AMP

Whilst shepherding was an essential part of life for the Children of Israel all throughout history, in the times preceding Jesus' birth, the status of shepherds had plummeted to where they were considered to be the bottom of society, only fit for roughing it out in the fields, looking after the sheep of some wealthy owner. For more information on this, have a look at:

https://www.epm.org/resources/2008/Mar/11/shepherds-status/

On the night of Jesus' birth, the shepherds who were keeping watch over their flock were no doubt a motley crew of rough looking men, but they had a job to do and they were faithfully and obediently doing it. They were keeping watch to protect the sheep from harm. They were loyal shepherds looking after their earthly master's sheep. It is quite significant that God saw their simple obedient hearts and chose **them** to reveal His great news of the birth of the Saviour, Jesus Christ the Lord! They were utterly startled and terrified at the appearance of the angel of the Lord, but what a privilege and a blessing it must have been to them. As we know from the rest of the story (verses 13-20) they went straight to the place where He was born and were the first to set eyes on the Saviour.

Now let's move ahead to Jesus' search for His first shepherds. When Jesus began His ministry, He was looking for those who would follow Him. What He taught them would become what they would then teach others. Jesus says of Himself that He is the Way, the Truth and the Life, and so that means His Words are the Way, the Truth and the Life. His whole life, ministry and teaching was to be the foundation on which His followers were to base their own lives.

Jesus chose twelve men to be His first disciples. They followed Him closely for 3 years, listening to His every Word, and seeking clarification if they did not understand what He was teaching them. As we know, one of these men, Judas Iscariot, betrayed Jesus, and another man, Matthias, was appointed to take Judas' place.

After Jesus was crucified, buried, raised from the dead and ascended into heaven, fifty days later - on the Day of Pentecost - Jesus poured out the Holy Spirit upon all those who were waiting in Jerusalem, where Jesus had told them to go. Acts Chapter 2 tells us that in the place that they were staying, they were all filled with the Holy Spirit, and began to speak in tongues, in different languages which they had not learnt, so that all in the crowds around could hear them praising and glorifying God in these different languages, as there were people there from many nations. With this infilling of the Holy Spirit, they were all given power from on high, and Peter began to preach the Word of God with boldness, telling the crowds what they must do to be saved; that they must repent and be baptized in the name of Jesus Christ for the forgiveness of their sins, and flee from this corrupt generation. This teaching was for them, and for all peoples to come.

That very day, the Church was born. Those twelve disciples became the twelve apostles, the **first shepherds** of God's Church. Yes, there were watchmen over God's chosen people, the Children of Israel, in the Old Testament times, but Jesus' twelve disciples (including Matthias) were God's first **watchmen** over His newly formed Church of those who believed in His son Jesus Christ. The New Testament is full of their godly teachings, all of which uphold everything that Jesus taught them whilst He was on the earth.

The role of God's shepherds has always been to keep watch over the flock and feed them with the truth of God's Word. Before He was crucified, three times Jesus said to Peter, "Do you love Me? … **Feed my sheep.**" (see John 21:15-17).

The role of a natural shepherd is to get the sheep to know the sound of his voice so that they will automatically follow him when he calls. His role is to protect the flock and steer them away from danger and keep them safe from attack by wild animals. The purpose of God's shepherds is to do the same; to get the flock (believers) to know the voice of their True Shepherd, Jesus Christ, so that they will follow Him, and obey His teachings at all times. Their role is to steer the sheep away from the dangers of the ways of the world, and to ensure that they are fed with sound, godly teaching; preaching the Gospel, baptising believers, discipling them into right living, and making sure believers are watchful and ever ready for the sudden return of Christ. God's shepherds are meant to be the 'watchmen at the gate', protecting and defending the flock so that they will not be led astray by the deceit of wolves (false teachers) coming in amongst them dressed up in sheep's clothing, having the appearance of a real shepherd of God.

The Rev Dr Clifford Hill, in his eye-opening book, *The Reshaping of Britain – Church and State since the 1960s: A Personal Reflection,* says,

*'The 'watchman' is not simply an observer of what is happening, but there has to be **understanding** of the significance of events and what needs to be done in response.'* [1]

Jesus warned His followers that wolves would come in amongst them to deceive them (see Matthew 7:15). The wolf doesn't come in amongst the sheep for a bit of light fun; he is out to kill, steal and destroy the flock (see John 10:10)!

The role of God's shepherds in the Old Testament

Let's look at a few Scriptures that show us God's view of the role of His shepherds, which at that time was His will in relation to the care and protection that He required of His chosen people, the Children of Israel. It equally applies to God's shepherds over His Church today.

"And I will give you shepherds after my own heart, who will guide you with knowledge and understanding." – Jeremiah 3:15

"Then I will appoint responsible shepherds who will care for them, and they will never be afraid again." – Jeremiah 23:4(a)

"Son of man, I have appointed you as a watchman for Israel. Whenever you receive a message from me, warn people immediately." – Ezekiel 3:17

"Once again a message came to me from the LORD: "Son of man, give your people this message: 'When I bring an army against a country, the people of that land choose one of their own to be a watchman. When the watchman sees the enemy coming, he sounds the alarm to warn the people. Then if those who hear the alarm refuse to take action, it is their own fault if they die. They heard the alarm but ignored it, so the responsibility is theirs. If they had listened to the warning, they could have saved their lives. But if the watchman sees the enemy coming and doesn't sound the alarm to warn the people, he is responsible for their captivity. They will die in their sins, but I will hold the watchman responsible for their deaths.'

"Now, son of man, I am making you a watchman for the people of Israel. Therefore, listen to what I say and warn them for me. If I announce that some wicked people are sure to die and you fail to tell them to change their ways, then they will die in their sins, and I will hold you responsible for their deaths. But if you warn them to repent and they don't repent, they will die in their sins, but you will have saved yourself." – Ezekiel 33:1-9

The Role and Qualifications of God's shepherds for the Church in the New Testament

Paul gives us a list of some of the leadership roles that are found within the Church and tells us what the purposes of these roles are for. This ends with a word of caution to the sheep concerning false teachers.

"And [His gifts to the church were varied and] He Himself appointed some as apostles [special messengers, representatives], some as prophets [who speak a new message from God to the people], some as evangelists [who spread the good news of salvation], and some as pastors and teachers [to shepherd and guide and instruct], [and He did this] to fully equip and perfect the saints (God's people) for works of service, to build up the body of Christ [the church]; until we all reach oneness in the faith and in the knowledge of the Son of God, [growing spiritually] to become a mature believer, reaching to the measure of the fullness of Christ [manifesting His spiritual completeness and exercising our spiritual gifts in unity]. ***So that we are no longer children [spiritually immature], tossed back and forth [like ships on a stormy sea] and carried about by every wind of [shifting] doctrine, by the cunning and trickery of [unscrupulous] men, by the deceitful scheming of people ready to do anything [for personal profit]."*** – Ephesians 4:11-14 AMP (Authors' emphasis)

On the basis that the shepherds **were** faithful and obedient to God's Word, the writer to the Hebrew believers gives the following instruction to the sheep:

"Obey your [spiritual] leaders and submit to them [recognizing their authority over you], for they are keeping watch over your souls and continually guarding your spiritual welfare as those who will give an account [of their stewardship of you]." – Hebrews 13:17(a) AMP

We can see from this that the role of God's shepherds is to keep watch over our souls as they will have to give an account to God on Judgement Day for the way they cared for us according to His Word. The shepherds are meant to feed us and nourish us with the uncompromising truth of God's Word, confronting us when we are in sin, exhorting us to live faithful and obedient lives in accordance with His Word, and keeping us on the narrow path that leads to eternal life. They hold a high position for which great judgement will fall on them if they lead the flock astray.

Paul told Timothy that,

"Every Scripture is God-breathed (given by His inspiration) and profitable for instruction, for reproof and conviction of sin, for correction of error and discipline in obedience, [and] for training in righteousness (in holy living, in conformity to God's will in thought, purpose, and action), so that the man of God may be complete and proficient, well fitted and thoroughly equipped for every good work." – 2 Timothy 3:16-17 AMPC

Below, Paul's instructions to Timothy concerning his role as a minister are a solemn, inescapable command; it is a holy charge which every church leader is expected to understand and obey. But do they? Where are such watchmen today?

"I solemnly charge you in the presence of God and of Christ Jesus, who is to judge the living and the dead, and by His appearing and His kingdom: preach the Word [as an official messenger]; be ready when the time is right and even when it is not [keep your sense of urgency, whether the opportunity seems favorable or unfavorable, whether convenient or inconvenient, whether welcome or unwelcome]; correct [those who err in doctrine or behavior], warn [those who sin], exhort and encourage [those who are growing toward spiritual maturity], with inexhaustible patience and [faithful] teaching." – 2 Timothy 4:1-2 AMP

Below is The Amplified Bible Classic Edition version:

"Herald and preach the Word! Keep your sense of urgency [stand by, be at hand and ready], whether the opportunity seems to be favorable or unfavorable. [Whether it is convenient or inconvenient, whether it is welcome or unwelcome, you as preacher of the Word are to show people in what way their lives are wrong.] And convince them, rebuking and correcting, warning and urging and encouraging them, being unflagging and inexhaustible in patience and teaching."

It would appear that much of the Church today does not like any aspect of these passages.

J.C. Ryle was the first Bishop of Liverpool from 1880 until his death in 1900. His evangelical ministry in the Anglican Church spanned fifty-eight years. We have many of his books, and they are filled to overflowing with convicting biblical truth. On the subject of the duties of a faithful minister, and referring to the account in Mark 6:14-29 of John the Baptist confronting King Herod, Ryle says,

'A faithful minister of God ought boldly to rebuke sin. John the Baptist spoke plainly to Herod about the wickedness of his life. He did not excuse himself under the plea that it was imprudent, or impolitic, or untimely, or useless to speak out. He did not say smooth things, and palliate the king's ungodliness by using soft words to describe his offence. He told his royal hearer the plain truth regardless of the consequences (v.18).

Here is a pattern that all ministers ought to follow. Publicly and privately, from the pulpit and in private visits, they ought to rebuke all open sin and deliver a faithful warning to all who are living in it. It may give offence. It may entail immense unpopularity.... If he believes a man is injuring his soul he ought surely to tell him so... How bitterly people hate a reprover when they are determined to keep their sins! ... When men and women have chosen their own wicked way they dislike anyone who tries to turn them.' [2]

It doesn't matter how people may react or respond; the shepherd must still do his God-ordained job of applying godly counsel, discipline and correction. That is his primary calling. The shepherd is like a parent training up their child to obey and do what is right. The child may not like it, but a good parent will fulfil their role regardless of the tears and tantrums of their wilfully rebellious child. Might we remind church leaders who are unwilling to heed God's Holy Word in this respect, that they will have to answer to God, and not to man, for their wilful disregard of His expectations of them and His instructions to them?

Concerning the qualifications of those who should be considered suitable for appointment to the role of shepherding God's people, Paul gives these eye-opening instructions to Timothy:

"This is a faithful and trustworthy saying: if any man [eagerly] seeks the office of overseer (bishop, superintendent), he desires an excellent task. ***Now an overseer must be blameless and beyond reproach, the husband of one wife****, self-controlled, sensible, respectable, hospitable, able to teach, not addicted to wine, not a bully nor quick-tempered and hot-headed, but gentle and considerate, free from the love of money [not greedy for wealth and its inherent power—financially ethical]. He must manage his own household well, keeping his children under control with all dignity [keeping them respectful and well-behaved] (for if a man does not know how to manage his own household, how will he take care of the church of God?). and He must not be a new convert, so that he will not [behave stupidly and] become conceited [by appointment to this high office] and fall into the [same] condemnation incurred by the devil [for his arrogance and pride]. And he must have a good reputation and be well thought of by those outside the church, so that he will not be discredited and fall into the devil's trap. Deacons likewise must be men worthy of respect [honorable, financially ethical, of good character],* ***not double-tongued [speakers of half-truths]****, not addicted to wine, not greedy for dishonest gain, but* ***upholding and fully understanding the mystery [that is, the true doctrine] of the [Christian] faith with a clear conscience [resulting from behavior consistent with spiritual maturity]. These men must first be tested; then if they are found to be blameless and beyond reproach [in their Christian lives], let them serve*** *as deacons."* – 1 Timothy 3:1-10 AMP (Authors' emphasis)

Important note: This passage says that the overseer **must be** the husband of one wife. Not the husband of a husband. Not the wife of a husband. Not the wife of a wife.

Paul then gives further instructions to Timothy about appointing people into leadership and also what to do with those in authority who continue in sin:

"As for those [elders] who continue in sin, reprimand them

in the presence of all [the congregation], so that the rest will be warned. I solemnly charge you in the presence of God and of Christ Jesus and of His chosen angels that you guard and keep these rules without bias, doing nothing out of favoritism. Do not hurry to lay hands on anyone [ordaining and approving someone for ministry or an office in the church, or in reinstating expelled offenders]*, and thereby share in the sins of others; keep yourself free from sin...* ***The sins of some people are conspicuous, leading the way for them into judgment [so that they are clearly not qualified for ministry]****; but the sins of others appear later [for they are hidden and follow behind them]."* – 1 Timothy 5:20-22, 24 AMP (Authors' emphasis)

Paul also gives similar instruction to Titus concerning the appointment of elders and overseers, and again in the Amplified translation, it reveals some very serious qualifications, which in today's Church are being discarded as if they are a nuisance.

"For this reason I left you behind in Crete, so that you would set right what remains unfinished, ***and appoint elders in every city as I directed you, namely, a man of unquestionable integrity, the husband of one wife, having children who believe, not accused of being immoral or rebellious. For the overseer, as God's steward, must be*** *blameless, not self-willed, not quick-tempered, not addicted to wine, not violent, not greedy for dishonest gain [but financially ethical]. And he must be hospitable [to believers, as well as strangers],* ***a lover of what is good, sensible (upright), fair, devout, self-disciplined [above reproach—whether in public or in private]. He must hold firmly to the trustworthy Word [of God] as it was taught to him, so that he will be able both to give accurate instruction in sound [reliable, error-free] doctrine and to refute those who contradict [it by explaining their error]."*** – Titus 1:5-9 AMP (Authors' emphasis)

For clarification, The Amplified Bible footnotes for church leaders says:

"The words *elder, overseer, and bishop* are used interchangeably to indicate the spiritually mature men who were qualified and selected to serve as leaders and shepherds over the church of God."

Shining a Spotlight

Let's take a moment to shine a spotlight on this: Church leaders are supposed to be **spiritually mature men,** who are qualified and selected to serve as leaders and shepherds over the Church of God. What sort of qualifications is this referring to? Are these qualifications the accolades that are accrued over years of study to impress others with our religious knowledge? No, the qualifications that are required for such leaders are all the biblical qualifications mentioned in the passages above, namely 1 Timothy 3:1-10 NLT and Titus 1:5-9 AMP. Today, many church leaders do not fit this description or meet these qualifications. Take a good look online at various churches around the world and you will see that many show no concern or regard to obeying God's Word on the serious appointment of its leaders. They appear to be happy to ignore or overlook God's criteria, preferring to decide for themselves whom they will appoint to the many varied positions in the Church, including the higher overseeing offices of archdeacon, deacon, area dean, dean, canon, vicar, and church warden; even archbishops seem to be usurping God's specifications when choosing whom to appoint as a bishop.

They seem to think that God is in agreement with their methods and policies of appointing leaders, but do you think that this rebellion is acceptable in God's eyes? Here is what God's Word says about it:

*"**They profess to know God** [to recognize and be acquainted with Him], **but by their actions they deny and disown Him. They are detestable and disobedient and worthless for good work of any kind.**"* – Titus 1:16 AMP (Authors' emphasis)

Disobedience is rebellion. If leaders are rebelling against God's Word, doesn't His Word say that rebellion is as witchcraft? (see 1

Samuel 15:23). If God sees it this way, what is the eternal destiny of all who are rebellious? (see Revelation 21:8). To know what God's Word says on these things, but to totally reject them, must surely be the height of pride and arrogance. Furthermore, if someone knows that they personally do not meet God's requirements and qualifications for church leadership, they should humbly admit it and decline the appointment. But to accept an appointment knowing that they do not meet the qualifications, and then go through a holy, solemn ceremony in the presence of God and a whole church full of witnesses, making holy vows with their hand on the Bible, is to take up a holy office based on a lie.

Jesus Himself tells us of the eternal destiny of those who love to live a lie:

"Outside the city are the dogs—the sorcerers, the sexually immoral, the murderers, the idol worshipers, ***and all who love to live a lie."*** – Revelation 22:15 (Authors' emphasis)

The 'city' is heaven. Anything that is 'outside the city' is in hell.

If we are a leader of a church and are living a life that is a lie, a life that is contrary to God's Holy Word, then let us not kid ourselves that we are safe simply because we hold a high office in the church. God is not mocked. Concerning those who profess to be believers, who have become entangled in unrepentant sin after having declared themselves to be a follower of Christ, Peter warns that,

"It would be better if they had never known the way to righteousness than to know it and then reject the command they were given to live a holy life." – 2 Peter 2:21

Hiding behind Robes

If we hold a position of high office in the Church, wearing elaborate robes is not a sign of our fitness for the role. We don't mean this in any disrespectful way; indeed, it is right to wear the robes of spiritual authority when we do so with integrity. What we mean is that some may use the wearing of these robes to hide a multitude of their own unrepentant sins, and also use them to assert a controlling influence over the flock to submit to ungodly, deceptive teaching.

If our heart and mind are not faithfully obeying God's Word, our robes of office will be like filthy rags to the Lord. On the Day of Judgement, we will walk around naked and ashamed for not having kept ourselves spiritually awake, prepared and ready for the Lord's return (see Revelation 16:15 AMP). The only robe that will give us entry into the kingdom of heaven is the robe that has been washed in the blood of the Lamb:

"Blessed (happy, prosperous, to be admired) are those who wash their robes [in the blood of Christ by believing and trusting in Him—the righteous who do His commandments], so that they may have the right to the tree of life, and may enter by the gates into the city." – Revelation 22:14 AMP

As we can see, God takes the role of His shepherds **very seriously**. He is desperate for His flock to be protected and brought safely into His eternal fold (the kingdom of heaven). Leaders of the Church should **not** take their position lightly. If they say they love God, they are supposed to feed His sheep (see John 21:15-17), not use their authority to further their own agenda. They are appointed to further God's will, which is to keep the sheep safe and fed with His Word so that they grow in faith and in obedience to it. The eternal destiny of the sheep is at stake, and how the shepherds handle their role is a matter of eternal life or death.

Knowing better than God?

Many respected, God-fearing friends and acquaintances concur with us that there is an alarming increase in the number of people taking up holy orders, who **no longer** accept as fact the things pertaining to God's Word and His commands because they believe they 'know better'. Reverence and obedience to what God says is viewed as something that can be opted out of and replaced with their own inventions of Christianity. Some refer to it as the Church coming under the control of the spirit of the age, which, in a nutshell, is outright demonic attack. Arrogance, hedonism and narcissism are now not only the domain of secular culture. Based on what we see happening within certain Church denominations, these ungodly beliefs, behavioural traits and practices have been taken on board by Church hierarchy and have formed a stronghold over the lives of many in leadership.

Here are some of Ryle's words concerning the implementing of additional inventions by those in positions of Church authority in his era, concluding with what is inevitably the end result of thinking that we 'know better than God'. Considering this was written over 150 years ago, this really ought to shout loudly to us today:

'Man's inventions in religion have a tendency to supplant God's Word... This was the state of things which our Lord found when he was on the earth. Practically the traditions of man were everything and the Word of God was nothing at all. Obedience to the traditions constituted true religion. Obedience to the Scriptures was lost sight of altogether... But there is a tendency in all religious institutions of mere human authority to usurp the authority of God's Word. In due course these very observances have been enjoined with more vigour than God's commandments and defended with more zeal than the authority of God's own Word. Church history is full of examples of this very procedure. Traditions are first called useful. Then they become necessary. At last they are too often made idols and all must bow down to them or be punished.' [3]

In addition, Hill's book, *The Reshaping of Britain – Church and State since the 1960s: A Personal Reflection* shines a spotlight on this subject brilliantly, and we will quote some of his work further. He skilfully gives a background as to **why** the Church is where it is today. We believe it is vital for all Christians to understand the past in order to make sense of what is happening in the Church in our times, but it is not the scope of our book to go into that detail. We would strongly encourage you to read Hill's book.

So, if we are in a leadership role but we do not meet the biblical criteria or are unfit in any way to hold that position, let us humble ourselves and do the right thing of resigning from our role, and then repent of our sin. This is honourable in the sight of God, and we will receive His forgiveness (see 1 John 1:8-10). But if we fail to do so, God's wrath and judgement awaits, which we will reveal in Chapter 5.

Let the seriousness of the role of God's shepherd sink in.

Chapter 2

THE RISE OF THE WOLVES

"I know that false teachers, like vicious wolves, will come in among you after I leave, not sparing the flock. ***Even some men from your own group will rise up and distort the truth in order to draw a following.*** *Watch out!"* – Acts 20:29-31(a) (Authors' emphasis)

"Children, it is the last hour [the end of this age]; and just as you heard that the antichrist is coming [the one who will oppose Christ and attempt to replace Him], even now many antichrists (false teachers) have appeared, which confirms our belief that it is the last hour. They went out from us ***[seeming at first to be Christians], but they were not really of us [because they were not truly born again and spiritually transformed]****; for if they had been of us, they would have remained with us;* ***but they went out [teaching false doctrine], so that it would be clearly shown that none of them are of us.****"* – 1 John 2:18-19 AMP (Authors' emphasis)

Knowing that Jesus said wolves would come in amongst us or even rise up from within the Church itself, we can see that they are most certainly in our midst today. But with His clear warning to be on our guard against it, how have we ever let this happen? Why have our shepherds opened the gate and let these wolves in to destroy us?! In the natural world, once a wolf is in amongst the sheep, its intent is to kill as many as possible, if not the entire flock. We have discovered from research that the only way it can be stopped is to be shot, although under European law, wolves are protected. The flock are powerless against a wolf, and so when one approaches, the natural instinct of the sheep is to scatter in every direction in order to survive. That is why the shepherd is appointed over them, to keep them all together and protect them from harm, and not to leave the gate open for wolves to come in amongst them with their slaughterous intent. This describes perfectly what is happening in the Church today. The only thing is that we can't go around shooting those who are wolves in sheep's clothing! The only option we have is to scatter without hesitation when we discern that a wolf has appeared on the scene.

Jesus says of His Church shepherds,

"Anyone refusing to walk through the gate into a sheepfold, who sneaks over the wall, must surely be a thief! For a shepherd comes through the gate. The gatekeeper opens the gate for him, and the sheep hear his voice and come to him; and he calls his own sheep by name and leads them out. He walks ahead of them; and they follow him, for they recognize his voice. They won't follow a stranger but will run from him, for they don't recognize his voice." – John 10:1-5 TLB

In this passage, Jesus is the Gatekeeper. He opens 'the gate' of the sheepfold to let in His shepherds to look after the sheep. Those shepherds who have come in through the gate (which is by having faith in Jesus and obedience to His Word) are true shepherds who will lead His sheep, and they will follow Him because they hear and recognise His voice. If someone proclaiming to be one of God's shepherds enters the fold through **another** way other than through the gate of **genuine faith and obedience** to God's Word, Jesus is saying that these people are thieves, and the sheep will flee.

On this subject, Ryle has something to say. It is the sort of preaching rarely heard from the pulpits of our churches today, which is clear evidence that we are in the time of the rise of the wolves. In his quote, he used the King James Version of the verses in the passage of Scripture we mentioned above. He does not mince his words, and we are left with a reality that we cannot escape:

'We have, for one thing, in these verses a vivid picture of a false teacher of religion. Our Lord says that he is one who 'enters not by the door into the sheepfold, but climbs up some other way'... The true sense of the 'door' must be sought in our Lord's own interpretation. It is Christ himself who is 'the door'. The true shepherd of souls is he who enters the ministry with a single eye to Christ, desiring to glorify Christ, doing all in the strength of Christ, preaching Christ's doctrine, walking in Christ's steps and labouring to bring men and women to Christ. The false shepherd of souls is he who enters the ministerial office with little or no thought about Christ, from worldly and self-exalting motives, but from no desire to exalt Jesus and the great salvation that is in him. Christ, in one word, is the grand touchstone of the minister of religion. The man who makes much of Christ is a pastor after God's own heart, whom God delights to honour. The minister who makes little of Christ is one whom God regards as an imposter, as one who has climbed up to his holy office not by the door, but by 'some other way'.

Thousands of ordained men in the present day know nothing whatever about Christ, except his name. They have not entered 'the door' themselves and they are unable to show it to others.

Unconverted ministers are the dry-rot of the church.' [1]

Hired Hands

As we begin this sub-section, we would like to ask you to read a number of Scriptures which we have set out over the next few pages. We would encourage you not to skip them as God's Word is vital, and only by reading Scripture upon Scripture will we be able to grasp that He means what He says. Where we have become sleepy, complacent or compromising in our work for the Lord, reading God's Word has the power to wake us up to His truth so that we can change our ways.

Jesus would describe many of our Church leaders as 'hired hands' who will run when they see the wolf coming after the sheep.

He says,

"I am the good shepherd. The good shepherd sacrifices his life for the sheep. A hired hand will run when he sees a wolf coming. He will abandon the sheep because they don't belong to him and he isn't their shepherd. And so the wolf attacks them and scatters the flock. The hired hand runs away because he's working only for the money and doesn't really care about the sheep." – John 10:11-13

The apostle Peter describes false teachers like this:

"But there were also false prophets in Israel, just as there will be false teachers among you. They will ***cleverly teach destructive heresies*** *and even deny the Master who bought them. In this way, they will bring sudden destruction on themselves. Many will follow their evil teaching and shameful immorality. And because of these teachers,* ***the way of truth will be slandered. In their greed they will make up clever lies to get hold of your money.*** *But God condemned them long ago, and their destruction will not be delayed."* – 2 Peter 2:1-3 (Authors' emphasis)

"These false teachers are like unthinking animals, creatures of instinct, born to be caught and destroyed. They scoff at things they do not understand, and like animals, they will be destroyed. Their destruction is their reward for the harm they have done. ***They love to indulge in evil pleasures in broad daylight. They are a disgrace and a stain among you. They delight in deception even as they eat with you in your fellowship meals. They commit adultery with their eyes, and their desire for sin is never satisfied. They lure unstable people into sin, and they are well trained in greed.*** *They live under God's curse."* – 2 Peter 2:12-14 (Authors' emphasis)

"These people are as useless as dried-up springs or as mist blown away by the wind. They are doomed to blackest darkness. ***They brag about themselves with empty, foolish boasting. With an appeal to***

twisted sexual desires, they lure back into sin those who have barely escaped from a lifestyle of deception. They promise freedom, but they themselves are slaves of sin and corruption. *For you are a slave to whatever controls you. And when people escape from the wickedness of the world by knowing our Lord and Savior Jesus Christ and then get tangled up and enslaved by sin again, they are worse off than before.* ***It would be better if they had never known the way to righteousness than to know it and then reject the command they were given to live a holy life."*** – 2 Peter 2:17-21 (Authors' emphasis)

"Most importantly, ***I want to remind you that in the last days scoffers will come, mocking the truth and following their own desires.*** *They will say, "What happened to the promise that Jesus is coming again? From before the times of our ancestors, everything has remained the same since the world was first created."...But the day of the Lord will come as unexpectedly as a thief. Then the heavens will pass away with a terrible noise, and the very elements themselves will disappear in fire, and the earth and everything on it will be found to deserve judgment.* ***Since everything around us is going to be destroyed like this, what holy and godly lives you should live,*** *looking forward to the day of God and hurrying it along. On that day, he will set the heavens on fire, and the elements will melt away in the flames. But we are looking forward to the new heavens and new earth he has promised, a world filled with God's righteousness.* ***And so, dear friends, while you are waiting for these things to happen, make every effort to be found living peaceful lives that are pure and blameless in his sight."*** – 2 Peter 3:3-4, 10-14 (Authors' emphasis)

Concerning the difficult words of some of Paul's letters, Peter says,

"Some of his comments are hard to understand, ***and those who are ignorant and unstable have twisted his letters to mean something quite different, just as they do with other parts of Scripture. And this will result in their destruction.*** *You already know these things,*

dear friends. ***So be on guard; then you will not be carried away by the errors of these wicked people and lose your own secure footing.*** *"* – 2 Peter 3:16(b) -17 (Authors' emphasis)

Jude writes:

"For certain people have crept in unnoticed [just as if they were sneaking in by a side door]. They are ungodly persons *whose condemnation was predicted long ago,* ***for they distort the grace of our God into decadence and immoral freedom [viewing it as an opportunity to do whatever they want],*** *and deny and disown our only Master and Lord, Jesus Christ."* – Jude 4 AMP (Authors' emphasis)

"When these people eat with you in your fellowship meals commemorating the Lord's love, ***they are like dangerous reefs that can shipwreck you. They are like shameless shepherds who care only for themselves...*** *These people are grumblers and complainers,* ***living only to satisfy their desires. They brag loudly about themselves, and they flatter others to get what they want.*** *But you, my dear friends, must remember what the apostles of our Lord Jesus Christ predicted. They told you that* ***in the last times there would be scoffers whose purpose in life is to satisfy their ungodly desires. These people are the ones who are creating divisions among you. They follow their natural instincts because they do not have God's Spirit in them.*** *"* – Jude 12(a), 16-19 (Authors' emphasis)

The prophet Isaiah says,

"For the leaders of my people— the LORD's watchmen, his shepherds— are blind and ignorant. They are like silent watchdogs that give no warning when danger comes. *They love to lie around, sleeping and dreaming. Like greedy dogs, they are never satisfied.* ***They are ignorant shepherds, all following their own path and intent on personal gain.*** *"Come," they say, "let's get some wine and have a party. Let's all get drunk. Then tomorrow we'll do it again and have an even bigger party!""* – Isaiah 56:10-12 (Authors' emphasis)

This same passage in The Living Bible translation puts it with even more scathing emphasis, and from our own observations of churches around the world today, in some cases this is a very apt description of the state of things:

"For the leaders of my people—the Lord's watchmen, his shepherds—are all blind to every danger. They are featherbrained and give no warning when danger comes. *They love to lie there, love to sleep, to dream. And they are as greedy as dogs, never satisfied;* ***they are stupid shepherds*** *who only look after their own interest,* ***each trying to get as much as he can for himself from every possible source.*** *"Come," they say.* ***"We'll get some wine and have a party; let's all get drunk. This is really living; let it go on and on, and tomorrow will be even better!"*** – Isaiah 56:10-12 TLB (Authors' emphasis)

The prophet Jeremiah says,

"The shepherds of my people have lost their senses. They no longer seek wisdom from the LORD. Therefore, they fail completely, and their flocks are scattered." – Jeremiah 10:21 (Authors' emphasis)

"What sorrow awaits the leaders of my people—the shepherds of my sheep—for they have destroyed and scattered the very ones they were expected to care for," *says the LORD. Therefore, this is what the LORD, the God of Israel, says to these shepherds: "**Instead of caring for my flock and leading them to safety, you have deserted them and driven them to destruction.**"* – Jeremiah 23:1-2(a) (Author's emphasis)

The prophet Ezekiel describes such leaders as follows:

"Your leaders are like wolves who tear apart their victims. They actually destroy people's lives for money!" – Ezekiel 22:27

It is clear that shepherds who enter the ministry with the attitude of that of a hired hand are not really interested or concerned for the flock, but are in the business of leading churches for the title they will gain, the salary, and the positions they will hold in Church circles and society in general, with a focus on the next position to which they could be promoted. Many see the institutional Church as a corporate business where they can join and climb up the ladder to success. They may see it as a career venture, aiming for the high office of Bishop, rather than coming into the Church to fulfil God's will, humbly as a servant of Christ (see Matthew 20:26 & Mark 9:35).

Some are drawn in by the rather lengthy, grandiose title that will be bestowed on them at their ordination. These titles often sound very righteous and holy, but personally, we feel they seem somewhat out of place in Christianity where those in leadership are simply meant to be servants to the flock rather than drawing attention to their position.

In the natural working environment, when someone is hired for a job to lead a team of people, they may initially be interested in the welfare of their colleagues for a while, but often seek to rise further up the ranks, thus abandoning their team to someone else. This can happen in the Church, with the temptation to rise further up the ladder of hierarchy, with more prestige, privileges and benefits, often including substantial free housing. Our once simple desire to shepherd God's flock becomes swallowed up in a desire for self-progression and recognition as someone of importance. When we forget the reasons why we became a shepherd, and fall for the temptation to view our role as a career rather than a position appointed by God, we have crossed the line into that of a hired hand; no longer solely concerned for the sheep but more interested in our own religious career progress.

Judas

When we take our eyes off the sheep in our care, and instead focus on ourselves and what we can gain from our position in the church, the spirit of Satan is waiting in the background ready to pounce and enter into us, like he did with Judas Iscariot. The spirit of Satan – his enticing words based on distortions of God's Word – is what turns a once faithful shepherd into a wolf in sheep's clothing. Let's remember that Jesus called Judas to be one of His disciples. Judas spent three years by Jesus' side listening to His teachings. He would have gone everywhere with Jesus and the rest of the disciples, doing the work of the Lord. In effect, he was one of the original twelve shepherds. But at some point, Judas was enticed by personal gain, and at that moment Satan entered into his soul, causing him to betray Jesus to the high priest so that they could arrest and crucify the Saviour. After the incident, Judas suddenly realised what he had done, but rather than repenting of it in brokenness and godly sorrow, he hung himself (see Matthew 27:5). Whilst there is what seems to be a contradictory view on how Judas died, as given in Luke's account in Acts1:18, we would encourage you to read an excellent explanation of both Matthew's and Luke's accounts on a website, which clarifies the matter, bringing the two accounts together perfectly. The site is www.answersingenesis.org/contradictions-in-the-bible/how-did-judas-die/

Ryle writes convincingly on the account of Judas; of what can happen to someone who started out as one who is called by God but lets his position get the better of him, causing him to forget what his purpose is in the work of the Lord.

'Hardness appears in Judas Iscariot who, after being a chosen apostle and a preacher of the kingdom of heaven, turns out at last a thief and a traitor. So long as the world stands, this unhappy man will be a lasting proof of the depth of human corruption. That anyone could follow Christ as a disciple for three years, see all his miracles, hear all his teaching, receive at his hand repeated kindnesses, be counted an apostle and yet prove rotten at heart in the end – all this at first sight appears incredible and impossible! Yet the case of Judas shows plainly that the thing can be. Few things, perhaps, are so little realized as the extent of the fall of man.' [2]

The harrowing story of Judas is something we read with much sadness, even feeling sorry for him that he failed to repent and receive God's forgiveness, but instead killed himself. But in our reading of it, do we ever realise that it is entirely possible that such a situation could come upon **any** follower of Christ, and in particular those who are in high positions in the Church, to whom much has been given and of whom much is required by God? (see Luke 12:48). If it happened to Judas, one of Jesus' chosen disciples, then it could happen to **anyone** who professes to be a shepherd of God's sheep but who has taken their eyes off the purpose of their work and is operating in ignorance, deception or seeking their own gain.

When we desire self-progress, we are making our own goal the focus of our work for God, rather than feeding the needs of His flock. Our personal desires for career progression within the Church can cause us to do whatever we deem necessary to obtain a promotion. It will cause us to listen to and adopt the teachings of those who have appointed us; teachings which may be in conflict with God's Word. Somehow those in positions of church authority seem to be able to explain away their compromising beliefs, and justify their teachings as reflecting a 'new Christian culture' which they convince us needs to be embraced. When we cross over from being a true shepherd to that of a hired hand, we then allow other ministers into our churches who support and preach these contrary teachings. It is at this point that we have opened the gates and let in the wolves.

Paul sums this up very clearly:

"I urge you, brothers and sisters, to keep your eyes on those who cause dissensions and create obstacles or ***introduce temptations [for others] to commit sin, [acting in ways] contrary to the doctrine which you have learned. <u>Turn away from them</u>. For such people do not serve our Lord Christ, but their own appetites and base desires. By smooth and flattering speech they deceive the hearts of***

***the unsuspecting [the innocent and the naive].*"** – Romans 16:17-18 AMP (Authors' emphasis)

Once one wolf is in the fold, devouring the sheep with its 'smooth and flattering speech' (lies of Satan), more wolves will be invited in. At the advance of the first wolf, many sheep **will** have the sense to flee, but those sheep who hesitate and remain in the fold will come under the increasing influence of these wolves, to the point that they become desensitized to the deception, and gradually find themselves being convinced that these lies are now a new Christian truth. Paul puts this very clearly in his first letter to Timothy:

"But the [Holy] Spirit explicitly and unmistakably declares that in later times some will turn away from the faith, paying attention instead to deceitful and seductive spirits and doctrines of demons, [misled] by the hypocrisy of liars whose consciences are seared as with a branding iron [leaving them incapable of ethical functioning]," – 1 Timothy 4:1-2 AMP

Division

Without a doubt, being in a church with a wolf in charge is the most dangerous place any sheep can be. You will feel pressured and cornered to move forward with their 'new Christianity'. If you don't, you will be viewed as a divisive troublemaker, when in reality all you are doing is speaking up for God's truth and righteousness and standing firm on the Word of the Lord. Your objections will be viewed as bigoted and hateful, when what you are actually doing is speaking the unchanging Word of God concerning the things which they now oppose and intend to overrule and change to suit their itching ears.

Let's get this straight: division in the Church, of whatever denomination, is **not** caused by those who stand up for and uphold God's Word in the face of rising false doctrine. Division is caused by those who are attempting to enforce false teaching on the flock. The division comes when the sheep have to scatter and leave their church because of the agenda of compromise and apostasy being pushed upon them by those in authority (see Romans 16:17-18 and Jude 16-19).

They will gang together, as is the nature of a pack of wolves, and will snarl at the sheep with their religious superiority. They will intimidate the sheep with their 'knowledge' which they claim is a new revelation concerning God's Word about a whole host of biblical teachings which they have now taken offense at, no longer want to listen to, nor believe or obey, and have relegated them to the trash bin. They will forcefully dig their heels in to enforce their so-called new Christian teaching, rather than allow the Holy Spirit to convict them and bring them to repentance.

Concerning the state of the Church and its escalating desire of embracing the ways of society into the heart of Christianity, when in fact it should be shouting from the roof tops the need to stop what is happening and repent, Nicholas Paul Franks, author of *Body Zero – Radical Preparation for the Return of Christ* pulls no punches:

'The main diagnosis for the denominational Body of Christ is repentance: "Repent, for the kingdom of God is at hand." Anything less than this isn't salvation and anything different to this isn't Christian discipleship.

Think of it for a moment: so-called believers brazenly doing their own thing while appealing to socio-cultural-political trends for justification; 'ministers' of the gospel who neither believe the gospel they espouse nor the Man they're supposed to love; congregations led by ravenous wolves; human sexuality – as in Corinth – widely seen as the apex of human entitlement, and equality, the baseline of our identity; forms of feminism lurching beyond the needed emphasis on equal rights for all into a falsified narrative of patriarchal systems that do not exist; ugly activist allegiances with political agendas that unwittingly seek to destroy all of society; seedbeds of antichrist insanity planted and tended in our children's schools with political propaganda encouraging gender dysphoria and confused sexuality.

As such, our political leaders are literally signing off policies that equate to state-sponsored child abuse, and all the while, the Church struggles to even muster a whimper, leaving it to a handful of stalwarts who are ostracised and made out to be monsters.' [3]

We will write about some of the aspects Franks has mentioned, later on in this book.

Jeremiah was full of the wrath of the Lord at what he witnessed among God's chosen people, and like many other prophets, he tried to warn them, but they would not listen:

"To whom can I speak and give warning? Who will listen to me? Their ears are closed so they cannot hear. ***The Word of the LORD is offensive to them; they find no pleasure in it.*** *But I am full of the wrath of the LORD, and I cannot hold it in."* – Jeremiah 6:10-11(a) NIV

On the subject of church leaders no longer listening to God, in his book, *The Reshaping of Britain – Church and State since the 1960s: A Personal Reflection*, Rev Dr Clifford Hill reveals an eye-opening speech given by the late Dr Donald Coggan, Archbishop of Canterbury from 1974 to 1980, to a packed audience at Lambeth Palace:

'On 23 July 1978...Donald Coggan addressed the Lambeth Conference. There were 400 bishops and senior clerics of the worldwide Anglican Communion gathered in Canterbury. In his address Dr Coggan said:

'Some of you have given up believing that God still speaks to the church. God forgive us. We would not admit it; it would shock our congregations if we did. But we have stopped listening to God and our spiritual life has died on us, though we keep up the appearances and go through the motions.'

He added,

'But many in the congregations know that God does speak, and that he makes his mind known to his followers.'

This last statement showed that he recognised a greater level of faith in the pew than in the pulpit. This had been confirmed to him by the 27,000 letters he had received from ordinary people, some of whom had a greater faith than their vicars.' [4]

Dr Donald Coggan was among the first to discern that this was the case in the 1970's, and many in the Church today know this to be even more the case now! Despite what is happening in our churches, many sheep want to stay in the fold to try to gain control back from those who are now appearing to be wolves in sheep's clothing. In the natural world, have you ever seen a flock of sheep succeed in chasing out the wolf that has entered the fold to attack and destroy them? We must heed these lessons of nature and do what real sheep do – **flee** when the wolves come!

We are under no obligation whatsoever to remain in a church that has handed itself over to Satan and his demons. Why would God expect any follower of Christ to choose to stay in a church when the Holy Spirit has actually departed from it Himself?

Removal of the Lampstands

Jesus says to churches that fail to repent, that He Himself will 'remove their lampstand from their place amongst the churches' (see Revelation 2:5). A lampstand gives light. In the Church, this light is the light of the Holy Spirit that shines out to the world when believers are faithful, obedient followers of Christ. But when churches allow sin to enter the House of God and they remain unrepentant, Jesus has every right to remove the light of the Holy Spirit from them. In effect He snuffs out their lampstand. When the light, the warmth and the power of the Holy Spirit has been withdrawn, the church becomes an empty, cold and soulless building. Ministers may go through the motions of Christian services but if the Holy Spirit is not there, then their effort is nothing but paying lip-service to the Lord.

The following verse is Jesus' view of those who outwardly appear godly, but where the reality is the exact opposite:

"Alas for you, you hypocritical scribes and Pharisees! You are like white-washed tombs, which look fine on the outside but inside are full of dead men's bones and all kinds of rottenness. ***For you appear like good men on the outside—but inside you are a mass of pretence and wickedness."*** – Matthew 23:27 PHILLIPS (Authors' emphasis)

We have walked into churches where you can tangibly feel the presence of the Lord. We have also walked into churches that once felt alive but now feel dead, and a cold shiver has come over us. When the Holy Spirit has departed from a church because the shepherds have embraced the doctrines of demons, then a sense of coldness will fill the atmosphere. When a lampstand is snuffed out, darkness fills the space. Not just a physical darkness, but a spiritual darkness too. They become the whitewashed tombs; still looking like lovely churches on the outside, but because the life-giving Holy Spirit is no longer there, they are full of spiritual death, filth and corruption. Jesus gives churches warnings concerning their waywardness, and He gives them time to repent (see Revelation Chapters 2 and 3). He does not want to snuff out any church; He wants the people to be faithful and obedient to His Word so that they can be true witnesses in their communities. But when churches ignore Him and fail to repent after the warnings that He gives them, then He **will** take action and snuff them out.

Evil is now Good, and Good is now Evil

When wolves rise up in our midst, they teach the lies of Satan, telling the sheep that these teachings are now 'good' when in fact they are evil. But God's Word has a warning to those who do this:

"What sorrow for those who say that evil is good and good is evil, that dark is light and light is dark, that bitter is sweet and sweet is bitter. What sorrow for those who are wise in their own eyes and think themselves so clever." – Isaiah 5:20-21

Concerning this, Andrea Williams, the founder of Christian Concern, says,

'Humanity has always been skilled at confusing good and evil. Modern society is no different. It tells us that ***a wrong deed can be right if the majority declare it not to be wrong.****'* (Williams' emphasis) [5]

In many cases, the error in the teaching of false shepherds is very subtle and can be difficult to discern. For example, we are aware of one newly appointed senior churchman who claimed in a sermon that the parable of the sheep and the goats is all about social action and nothing to do with hell (see Matthew 25:31-46). When challenged about this, he chose not to explain his distorted teaching.

Many leaders have a focus on bringing people into their church by whatever means possible, hoping that Jesus will somehow 'rub off' on them and save their souls without them needing to hear any preaching about confession of sin or repentance. What these ministers say can sound so loving and godly, but when closely examined with the teaching of Scripture, it can be seen to be a deliberate twisting of the Word of God to suit their own agenda. Without exposing what is evil and sinful in the sight of God, and without preaching the need for confession and repentance, these ministers are leading people on the wide path to the place called hell; that place which Jesus teaches on more than any other subject, but which these ministers deny or refuse to preach about. Like the Pied-piper of Hamelin, everyone 'dances' to the tune that is being played by these leaders, causing them to follow wherever their leader may take them.

Paul warns believers about their gullibility when it comes to hearing teaching that comes from those who, unbeknown to them, are deceiving the flock. He says these people are servants of Satan, masquerading as ministers of righteousness.

"I am afraid that, even as the serpent beguiled Eve by his cunning,

your minds may be corrupted and led away from the simplicity of [your sincere and] pure devotion to Christ. For [you seem willing to allow it] if one comes and preaches another Jesus whom we have not preached, or if you receive a different spirit from the one you received, or a different gospel from the one you accepted. You tolerate all this beautifully [welcoming the deception]... For such men are counterfeit apostles, deceitful workers, masquerading as apostles of Christ. And no wonder, since Satan himself masquerades as an angel of light. So it is no great surprise if his servants also masquerade as servants of righteousness, but their end will correspond with their deeds." – 2 Corinthians 11:3-4 & 13-15 AMP

Paul also says,

"Let no one deceive you with empty arguments [that encourage you to sin], for because of these things the wrath of God comes upon the sons of disobedience [those who habitually sin]." – Ephesians 5:6 AMP

Remember, Satan had the audacity to twist the Word of God, speaking outright lies to Adam and Eve, enticing them to rebel against what God had forbidden them to do. As Satan's servants can masquerade as servants of righteousness, we must be on our guard for their appearance within the Church. Never believe or trust anyone in the Church who refutes or contradicts God's Word, for they are likely to be one of Satan's servants rather than one of God's.

When a church has been taken over by Satan's servants, unless they repent, God will not allow that church to remain in existence for long. Eventually it will collapse. Unless the Lord builds the house, they that try to build it labour in vain (see Psalm 127:1). If the Holy Spirit has left, and repentance is nowhere to be seen in a church, those who still try to run it can labour all they like, but their work will fail. Under the label of Christianity, they are attempting to build their new liberating, embracing 'church' based on lies, deception and unbelief, and God will not allow it to stand, as it is a grief to the Holy Spirit.

There is an excellent book concerning this, titled, *Witchcraft in the Pews* by George Bloomer.

If you are a follower of Christ and your church is being taken over by progressive, liberal ministers - from bishops right down to those who are members of church committees - who support and promote teachings that are diametrically opposed to what is clearly written in God's Word, then you can be sure that they are the wolves in sheep's clothing that Jesus is warning us about. Pick up your belongings, walk out of the building, and do not look back.

God will go with you and He will show you where to find a good shepherd.

"The LORD is my Shepherd [to feed, to guide and to shield me], I shall not want." – Psalm 23:1 AMP

Chapter 3

SCATTERING THE SHEEP

"The shepherds of my people have lost their senses. They no longer seek wisdom from the Lord. Therefore, they fail completely, and their flocks are scattered." – Jeremiah 10:21

In the passage below, the Old Testament priests were not honouring God because they did not obey the Law in many ways. Today, many Church leaders are not honouring God because they are disobeying and abandoning the teachings of Scripture. They are rebelling against the Word of God and are brazenly trying to redefine what is written. The result of this is that those who sit under the authority of these leaders are in danger.

"For the lips of the priest should guard and preserve knowledge [of My law], and the people should seek instruction from his mouth; for he is the messenger of the LORD of hosts. ***But as for you [priests], you have turned from the way and you have caused many to stumble by your instruction [in the law]."*** – Malachi 2:7-8(a) AMP (Authors' emphasis)

Generally speaking, a grazing flock of sheep will stick together, not straying far from one another. When a natural shepherd abandons his role of keeping watch over the flock, the sheep are unprotected, the wolves come in and the sheep run for their lives because they instinctively know that the wolf is not their shepherd. The whole flock will flee, but if any sheep have strayed from the flock, these are the ones that will be devoured by the wolf.

This is what we should expect to happen when an imposter rises up within the Church. If our leaders are abandoning their role of keeping us safe by feeding us with the uncompromising truth of the Word of God, and have let wolves in sheep's clothing in to lead us astray with false teachings, if we are truly tuned in to hearing the voice of our True Shepherd, Jesus Christ, we should run for our lives when we hear their lies coming from the pulpits. This may mean the whole flock leaving the church they have been a part of all their lives and relocating somewhere else.

We have reached a time where there is so much deception in the Church - designed for the purpose of making everyone feel welcome and comfortable in all their sins - that the sheep who are raising their voices in objection to it are now being silenced by their leaders, or are being pressured in subtle ways to get on board with the changing tide of the modern Church. Those in the congregations who refuse to accept this 'new Christianity' are made to feel that their determination to hold to the truth of Scripture is actually 'un-Christlike' and has even recently been termed as 'hate-speech'. One needs only to read updates of personal cases on websites such as www.christianconcern.com to see that this is a regular occurrence.

This kind of 'soft' Christianity may bring people in, but it fails in teaching them to confess and repent of their sins or obey God's Word. It is teaching them that God is okay with them remaining as they are; it pats them on the head with 'comforting words' that God loves them and wants them to be happy, and whatever they want to be in life, and however they wish to live it, then God is fine with it all. Confession, repentance and obedience to godly teaching are now seen as an obstacle that Church leaders want to remove, to make it easier for people to feel welcomed and comfortable. Come on Church, wake up! This is about as far removed from biblical teaching as it is ever possible to get! Quite obviously, the result of this 21st century 'Christianity' is that the faithful sheep who have been listening to and obeying the voice of the True Shepherd for decades, are now finding themselves treated as outcasts, and labelled as bigots.

Many leaders are remaining silent in the face of what is now happening within the Church, not speaking out one way or the other in the hope that their silence on all the issues will keep the trouble from their doors. To remain silent when we know that we should be speaking up and upholding the truth of God's Word against the torrent of deception and apostasy, is to actually condone the very things about which we are choosing to remain silent.

Where do the faithful sheep go when their leaders jump on the bandwagon of political correctness and adopt teachings that should never be present in the House of God? What do we do when those in high positions force upon us new leaders whose lifestyles are diametrically opposed to the biblical qualifications for those in positions of Church leadership? What do we do when our objections are 'listened to' but go unheeded? What do we do when we have spent much of our life in a church and given our heart and soul into it, not to mention the finances we may have sown into it? What do we do when we have given our all to follow Jesus, and now we are facing eviction from the House of God which was once the place we called 'Home'; our place of solace, nourishment and encouragement, where we were taught right from wrong from a biblical perspective, and where our shepherds used to preach the truth to us?

What Do we Do? …

We **flee from them!** We come out from under their compromising, deceptive teaching. To stay in the midst of it means that we are silently tolerating and agreeing with their teaching. We must literally grab ourselves by the scruff of the neck and force ourselves out of the building. This will be excruciating for many who have been faithful Christians in a particular church for many years. Many are not prepared to pack up and leave behind everything they have given their lives to. But we have reached a time where we can no longer just sit in the pews and hope to pray the problem away. Our prayers must be accompanied with acts of obedience. God's Word says to come out of it.

"Do not be unequally bound together with unbelievers [do not make mismatched alliances with them, inconsistent with your faith]. For what partnership can righteousness have with lawlessness? Or what fellowship can light have with darkness? What harmony can there be between Christ and Belial (Satan)? Or what does a believer have in common with an unbeliever? What agreement is there between the temple of God and idols? For we are the temple of the living God; ...So, come out from among [unbelievers], and separate (sever) yourselves from them, says the Lord, and touch not [any] unclean thing; then I will receive you kindly and treat you with favour. And I will be a Father to you, and you shall be My sons and daughters, says the Lord Almighty." – 2 Corinthians 6:14-16(a) AMP; 17-18 AMPC

Our loyalty is to God, not to our beloved church building, and there is one question we need to answer when faced with such a massive dilemma; a dilemma that is happening to more and more followers of Christ as the weeks, months and years go by.

The question is **"Who are we following?"**

Follow Me

In the Gospels, many times Jesus said, "Follow Me". In the following verse, Jesus makes it quite clear what He requires us to do if we profess to be one of His followers:

"If any of you want to be my follower, you must stop thinking about yourself and what you want. *You must be willing to carry the cross that is given to you for following me."* – Matthew 16:24 ERV (Authors' emphasis)

The Passion translation of this verse makes it deeply personal, targeting the very purpose of what it means to be a follower of Christ.

"Then Jesus said to his disciples, "If you truly want to follow me, ***you should at once completely reject and disown your own life. And you must be willing to share my cross and experience it as your own, as you continually surrender to my ways.*** *"* – Matthew 16:24 TPT (Authors' emphasis)

When we examine the life we live for Christ, and how we feel about the commitment we have made to the church that we may have been a member of for a long time, do we feel aggrieved at the prospect of giving it all up and being forced out of the door by the appointment of progressive, liberal wolves in sheep's clothing that are being foisted upon us in spite of our biblical objections? In the above verse, Jesus is clearly stating that if we **truly** want to follow Him, we must completely forsake what we personally want and be willing to share **His** cross and experience it as our own, and to continue to surrender to His ways. Sharing His cross does **not** mean staying in a church that is embracing deception and diluting Scripture, particularly if it has got to the point where what is going on within its walls could be considered to be a 'den of iniquity'.

So in the matter of what do we do when faced with the wolf that has been welcomed into our midst, Jesus is saying that we must forget all that we have invested into our church, pick up His cross (of rejection and persecution) and carry it as our own, and then follow Him, surrendering our own wants, desires and interests in order to follow His ways. His ways are to listen to His voice and **obey** His Father's Word.

"My sheep listen to my voice; I know them, and they follow me." – John 10:27

If our church leaders are no longer fulfilling their role to faithfully preach and teach obedience to the Word of God, and are now accepting, welcoming, embracing, and celebrating sin, throwing aside the very things that Jesus and the apostles taught concerning conviction, confession and repentance, then these leaders are no longer obeying and believing God's Word. True sheep hear the voice of the Shepherd (Jesus) and follow and obey Him. If we hear God's Word but fail to obey it, then the reality is we are **not** His sheep. So, when our leaders no longer believe sound doctrine, there is no other way of putting this... they are not His sheep and therefore they are **unbelievers**. We cannot proclaim to be a believer if we **do not** believe and obey God's Word.

If we are true sheep, standing in faith on God's Word, and are faced with being taken over by leaders who are now bowing their knee to unbiblical teaching, then we need to obey Jesus' command and follow Him, **not them!** Apostate leaders are **unbelievers** and we cannot be yoked together with them.

Just because a person has been appointed into a role by a bishop, or even by an archbishop, and is now wearing elaborate robes befitting their religious title, making them appear knowledgeable in the ways of the Lord, we must not be deceived by their outward appearance.

Ryle says,

'Ordination is no proof whatever that a man is fit to show others the way to heaven.' [1]

Again, he says,

'I may be allowed to say that none need warning so much as the ministers of Christ's gospel. Our office and our ordination are no security against errors and mistakes. It is, alas, too true that the greatest heresies have crept into the church of Christ by means of ordained men.' [2]

Many of today's church leaders are merely giving the outward expression of what it means to be the 'Church'; a great pretence is being played out as they honour God with their lips, yet their hearts are far from Him (see Matthew 15:8). They speak spiritual-sounding words but in the deepest recesses of their hearts all manner of unconfessed and unrepentant sin may be lurking or even festering. God sees behind the masks that people wear, especially when they are worn to deceive us. If a leader has been appointed in a manner that is contrary to the strict instruction laid down in God's Word, and if a leader's lifestyle is contrary to Scripture, if they refuse to repent of their sin and rebellion, then in God's eyes they are no longer a believer. A person cannot declare that they are a believer whilst at the same time **not believe and obey** the teachings of the One they say they profess to believe in. This is utter delusion!

At the risk of repeating ourselves, for the sheep who are caught in the crossfire of the arrival of wolves in sheep's clothing, as painful as the dilemma is, at the end of the day it is **Jesus** who we are to follow. We must not allow ourselves to remain under the headship of apostate leaders simply because of all that we have personally given over the years into a particular church. Jesus is our Shepherd. Our emotional attachment to a particular church must be forsaken when a spiritual crisis like this occurs, so that we can hear Jesus' voice and follow where He leads. If we are followers of Christ, and our leaders have given themselves over to heeding deceiving spirits and doctrines of demons (see 1 Timothy 4:1), we should not remain in our church for sentimental reasons.

Alarm Bells are Ringing!

If our home and all the lovely belongings that mean so much to us were on fire, we would get out of the building as fast as we could, not hang about in the flames hoping that we could somehow save it all. If a ship was sinking, we would jump into the lifeboats and row ourselves to safety quickly. Yet some in the church think that if they stay in their churches, they will somehow be able to overturn the deception. Putting your finger into a hole in a dam, hoping to stem the trickle that is seeping through the cracks, is not going to stop the dam from bursting. Behind that trickle is a great tsunami waiting to burst through and destroy everything in its path. We are now in the times where this is what the Church is facing. From the top downwards, the spirit of the antichrist is taking over the leadership of the House of God, and all the sheep in the fold are blissfully unaware that a tsunami of deception is about to swallow them up with its lies. When people rise up and blow the trumpet to warn them of impending catastrophe, we need to heed the warnings and take action.

The Great Shaking

There are leaders in many churches all around the world who teach deceptive doctrine - some of it being very openly opposed to God's Word - which they proudly preach without apology. More and more sheep are being scattered. They feel abandoned and alone, wondering where they are going to find shelter. Over the past 30 years, many churches have had weekly house groups for their congregation to attend. But more recently, we are hearing of 'churchless' scattered sheep getting together to form their own little house groups, just like it would have been in the early church. Those first Jewish followers of Christ were no longer welcome in their synagogues, and so they gathered together to worship God in each other's homes. Maybe God is shaking up the established Church to extract His faithful sheep out of an institution that is rapidly becoming the domain of Satan and his demons, and a lampstand that is about to be snuffed out.

A Word for Hesitant Sheep

Despite all that we have said in this chapter, if you are a 'hesitant sheep', still unsure of what to do with what you are facing within the church that you are attending, allow us to show you some passages of Scripture that we believe will help you make your mind up.

In the Old Testament, let's look at two accounts where righteous people found themselves surrounded by people who refused to repent of their sins.

A Summary of the story of Noah and his family (Genesis Chapters 6 & 7)

Noah was a righteous man whom God said was the only blameless person living on the earth at that time. Can you imagine what it must have been like for him to be the only person trying to uphold God's Word in a world that was full of people who were totally corrupt and full of violence? God told Noah that He was going to destroy all living things on the earth and the whole earth itself because of the evil that He saw. He told Noah to build a large boat to house him and his family, plus a pair (one male and one female) of every kind of creature. Noah did as God commanded and then they all went into the boat. God sent the rain upon the earth for forty days and forty nights destroying every living thing. The waters flooded the earth for 150 days. Nothing on the earth survived; only Noah and his family and all the creatures in the boat.

In the New Testament, Peter briefly refers to this story:

"And God did not spare the ancient world—except for Noah and the seven others in his family. ***Noah warned the world of God's righteous judgment.*** *So God protected Noah when he destroyed the world of ungodly people with a vast flood."* – 2 Peter 2:5 (Authors' emphasis)

A Summary of the story of Lot and his family (Genesis 18:20-33 & 19:1-29)

Lot had chosen to live in Sodom when he and Abraham had parted company due to the land not being able to sustain the size of their families and livestock (see Genesis Chapter 13). But the people of Sodom and Gomorrah lived corrupt and immoral lifestyles. Lot was tormented night and day with living in this godless environment, and he cried out to God. The Lord heard his cry and sent two angels to the entrance of the city of Sodom. Lot bowed down to them and welcomed them to stay with him. That evening, all the men of Sodom, both young men and old men came and surrounded Lot's house and shouted at Lot that they wanted to have sex with the two men (angels) who were staying with him. When Lot refused to let them commit such evil, the men of Sodom lunged at him in an attempt to break down the door, but the two angels pulled Lot back inside the house and bolted the door. The angels then blinded all the men who were outside the door.

The angels then told Lot to gather all his relatives and to get out of the city because God was about to destroy it due to the outcry against it. When Lot told his daughters' fiancés about what was going to happen, they thought he was just joking. The next day the angels became **insistent** that Lot take his wife and daughters and get them out immediately or they would be swept away in the destruction. Lot still hesitated, but the angels grabbed the hands of all of them and rushed them out of the city and ordered them to not look back. When Lot reached the nearby village of Zoar, God rained down fire and burning sulphur from the sky on Sodom and Gomorrah and the surrounding villages, wiping out all the people (including Lot's daughters' fiancés as they did not leave the place) and destroying absolutely everything. Lot's wife had been following on behind him, and despite being warned by the angels not to look back at the destruction that was occurring, she ignored their warning. As she looked back towards what she had left behind, she turned into a pillar of salt.

Peter refers to this story too, and describes in detail Lot's feelings about the environment he was living in:

"God condemned the cities of Sodom and Gomorrah and turned them into heaps of ashes. He made them an example of what will happen to ungodly people. ***But God also rescued Lot out of Sodom because he was a righteous man who was sick of the shameful immorality of the wicked people around him. Yes, Lot was a righteous man who was tormented in his soul by the wickedness he saw and heard day after day.*** *So you see, the Lord knows how to rescue godly people from their trials, even while keeping the wicked*

under punishment until the day of final judgment. He is especially hard on those who follow their own twisted sexual desire, and who despise authority." – 2 Peter 2:6-10a (Authors' emphasis)

God wants to rescue His faithful and obedient sheep out of the 'Sodom and Gomorrah' environments that some of our churches are gradually becoming. When God says to come out from amongst them (see 2 Corinthians 6:17), He means what He says, and we had better take action. We can't hang about in a church simply because it has been part of our life for so long and we love the building, the services, and the friends we have made there over the years. When demons have taken control of the doctrine, and our ministers begin to preach these lies, telling us that they are now 'updated Christian teachings' relevant to the world we now live in, we must scatter in every direction as fast as possible and **not look back** at what we are leaving. If we do look back, we may find ourselves being tempted by Satan to doubt our decision to leave, and then end up returning to the swamp of apostasy. We must follow the uncompromising Word of God and cling hard to it when all hell is breaking loose around us.

The Psalmist wrote:

*"**Blessed** [fortunate, prosperous, and favored by God] **is the man who does not walk in the counsel of the wicked [following their advice and example], Nor stand in the path of sinners, Nor sit [down to rest] in the seat of scoffers (ridiculers).** But his delight is in the law of the LORD, And on His law [His precepts and teachings] he [habitually] meditates day and night."* – Psalm 1:1-2 AMP (Authors' emphasis)

This is what the sheep must do! The desire of our heart should be to habitually immerse ourselves in the Word of God, and remove ourselves from following the advice and example of those who attempt to 'persuade' us that their counsel is godly, when the evidence from the Bible is that their teaching is the lie of Satan.

When we are forced to flee, God will see us, and He will take care of us.

"For this is what the Sovereign LORD says: I myself will search and find my sheep. I will be like a shepherd looking for his scattered flock. I will find my sheep and rescue them from all the places where they were scattered..." – Ezekiel 34:11-12

For the sake of our salvation, we really have no option. We must trust in God to lead us to safe pastures under the leadership of shepherds who are not prepared to compromise His Word. God will not abandon His faithful sheep, but He may have to cause them to scatter far and wide when the wolves have arrived to devour them.

Chapter 4

APOSTASY, DECEPTION AND HERESY

"See to it that no one takes you captive through philosophy and empty deception [pseudo-intellectual babble], according to the tradition [and musings] of mere men, following the elementary principles of this world, rather than following [the truth—the teachings of] Christ." – Colossians 2:8 AMP

"Let no one in any way deceive or entrap you, for that day will not come unless the apostasy comes first [that is, the great rebellion, ***the abandonment of the faith by professed Christians]****,..."* – 2 Thessalonians 2:3(a) AMP (Authors' emphasis)

"For [God does not overlook sin and] the wrath of God is revealed from heaven against ***all ungodliness and unrighteousness of men who in their wickedness suppress and stifle the truth****,.."* – Romans 1:18 AMP (Authors' emphasis)

Let's begin by having a look at what the words 'apostasy', 'deception' and 'heresy' mean.

The Google definition of the word 'apostasy' is *"the abandonment or renunciation of a religious (or political) belief or principle."*

The Google definition of the word 'deception' is *"the action of deceiving someone."*

The Google definition of the word 'heresy' is *"a belief or opinion contrary to orthodox religious (especially Christian) doctrine."*

In this chapter we will look at some of the things that are happening in the Church today that can be considered as apostasy; the abandonment or renunciation of God's Word, and thereby can be deemed to be deception and heresy. It must be remembered that any teaching that is being driven by Church leaders, which has an agenda, even in a subtle way, to move away from the preaching of sound doctrine as written in God's Word, means that such teaching is anti-biblical. Anything that is anti-biblical means that it is against Christ and His teachings. Anything that is against Christ is of the Antichrist. On this basis, it has to be concluded that anything being taught, especially within the Church, that is against Christ and against the Word of God, is therefore demonic, no matter how nicely we try to dress it all up to come across as being 'Christian'.

Many leaders today want Christianity to be based on the personal feelings and preferences of themselves and members of their congregations, rather than facing the fact that the Bible teaches us that our natural feelings of the flesh need changing through obedience to Biblical truth, thereby transforming us into the image of Christ. Jesus was sinless and pure. He was not a thief or a murderer; He was not sexually immoral in any way whatsoever, never using His body as an instrument of unrighteousness (see Romans 6:13). Therefore, being a follower of Christ means that we are to be like Him, conducting our lives in ways that display His likeness.

When genuine seekers look at us, they want to see Jesus in us. They want to see something radically different to what they see in this fallen, sinful world; they are searching for something that will save them from their own sins. If they see professing Christians, in particular Church leaders, living an unrepentant sinful life and not seeming to care about it, but rather openly and unashamedly promoting it, they will wonder what the point is in being a Christian at all if it doesn't do anything to rescue them from their sin. Quite rightly, they will view us as hypocrites, and because of our wilful rebellion, the way of truth will be slandered (see 2 Peter2 :2).

Concerning the religious leaders of the time and the way they were twisting God's Law for their own benefit, the Amplified Bible footnote for a particular verse describes this conduct as follows:

'The Pharisees were distorting and breaking God's law by giving their own interpretations priority over the plain meaning of the Scriptures.' - (footnote for Romans 2:23)

That description is the basis for the contents of this chapter. It is the distorting of the Scriptures, by those who are our shepherds, which we intend to expose. By no means is this chapter an extensive study on the issues. It is merely to highlight some of the things that are going on in our churches, under the authority and approval of our shepherds, which are obvious contraventions to what God's Word clearly says. No one who is deliberately living in a way that is contrary to God's Word likes to hear the truth, and will quite firmly resist and reject it, but nevertheless the truth stands for all to see, and will remain the truth for eternity, regardless of our personal objection to it. It should go without saying that to compromise and twist Scripture to suit our own personal desires and agendas is to deliberately abuse the Word of God.

The Root

To get the ball rolling, we need to understand how it is even possible for deception to occur in the hearts and minds of people who profess to be followers of Christ; we need to get to the root of the matter so that we can clearly see why our personal thoughts and beliefs can be wrong when held up to the light of God's Word. We all think that our **own** thoughts and views on Christian matters are right, even when the biblical truth is staring us in the face and exposing our thoughts as a lie. So, let's see how deception can start in the life of a believer.

Without our realising it, Satan sows a suggestion into our heart. We let the suggestion settle there, and we think about it over and over. At first, we may understand what God's Word says on a given matter, but as Satan's suggestion ferments and takes root in our heart, our mind begins to find ways to justify to our heart why it would be perfectly reasonable to pursue something that God says is wrong, or continue in it if we are already doing it. Fermentation is a process that works on something to convert it into something else. In the case of making wine, yeast is added to the grape juice and the process of fermentation spreads throughout the entire quantity of juice and changes it into wine. So, when the 'yeast' of deception gets into our hearts and minds and we allow it to ferment, it will change our godly thoughts into something else. Satan's 'whisperings' of suggestions are the 'yeast' which ferments in our mind, taking over our whole being and changing our godly thoughts into ones that are sinful.

In Matthew 16:5-12, Jesus talks of the leaven of the Pharisees and the Sadducees. Leaven is what we would know as yeast. In relation to that passage of Scripture, Ryle says,

'Our Lord calls their false doctrines 'leaven' (v.6). Like leaven, they may seem a small thing compared to the whole body of truth. Like leaven, once admitted they work secretly and noiselessly. Like leaven, they would gradually change the whole nature of the religion with which they are mixed. It was not just the open danger of heresy but the hidden!

This warning was meant for all time. Our Lord knew that Pharisee doctrines and Sadducee doctrines would prove the two great wasting diseases of his churches until the end of the world. We live in a world where Pharisaism and Sadduceeism are continually striving for the mastery in the church of Christ. Some want to add to the gospel and some want to take away from it. Some would bury it and some would pare it down to nothing. Some would stifle it by heaping on it additions and some would bleed it to death by subtraction from its truths. Both parties agree in only one respect. Both would kill and destroy the life of Christianity if they succeeded in having their own way. Against both errors let us watch and pray and stand guard. Let our principle be 'the truth, the whole truth and nothing but the truth', nothing added to it and nothing taken away.' [1]

The leaven of Satan's suggestions (lies) are the weapons he uses to cause us to eventually betray Jesus. Each time we side with his lies, we have fallen for his temptations in our thoughts and hearts. At some point, the suggestions which we have begun to accept will eventually play out in our actions. What we outwardly do is the result of a long process of what is going on in our mind and heart. We have to realise that when we allow deception into our minds and hearts, letting it ferment and change our godly thoughts into something else, stubbornly convincing ourselves with thoughts such as, "I don't believe what Jesus is saying about this", then march forward in our life based on our deceptive thoughts, then there is no other way of putting it; we are in blatant rebellion against God.

Having looked at the root of deception and how it occurs, we will now head into showing you examples of this in the Church today. Because of the subject matter of this chapter, it is quite long, so we have broken it down into various categories and then separated them out into four sections to make the whole chapter easier to read. We will write either in brief or at more length in accordance with what God's Word says, as our desire is to obey God and uphold Scripture. Michele wrote about many of these things in her book, *The Gospel of Deception – Counterfeit Christianity and the Fate of Its Followers*, but we have updated the text and added several other categories which have come to light in recent times.

Chapter 4 - Section A

Sexual Immorality; Women in Headship; God is 'female'

We will start, in the first section, with what is probably the most hotly debated subject in the Church today...

Sexual Immorality

Institutional sex abuse scandals; Sexuality and confusion; Same-sex relationships & same-sex 'marriage'; Unrepentant sexual immorality.

"Therefore ***do not let sin reign in your mortal body so that you obey its evil desires. Do not offer any part of yourself to sin as an instrument of wickedness****, but rather offer yourselves to God as those who have been brought from death to life; and offer every part of yourself to him as an instrument of righteousness."* – Romans 6:12-13 NIV (Authors' emphasis)

There is increasing discussion and debate on this subject in both Church and secular circles, all of which shows an intention to undermine and question the validity of the Word of God. However, as followers of Christ, **we** wish to make things very clear about what God's Word says on this immensely sensitive matter.

We will start by saying that, through Jesus' sacrifice on the cross, God's grace, mercy, and forgiveness for our sins has been made available for the whole human race, whatever our sins may be. We can receive His loving gifts to us this very day through confession and repentance of our sins, and following Christ by obeying His Word.

But there is a Day coming when this period of grace, mercy and forgiveness will cease. That 'Day' is known in the Bible as the Day of Judgement. God does not want anyone to perish but for all to come to repentance (see 2 Peter 3:9) before that fearful Day arrives, because that is the point when His grace, mercy and forgiveness will cease and His judgement must begin. Those who have given their lives to Christ and have repented of their sins will spend eternity in heaven; but those who have not will spend eternity with Satan in hell. The fact that many in the Church dispute this biblical truth (which is one of many they dispute) is part of the problem we are addressing in this book. As many a cynic might say, "Why let facts, or God's truth, stand in the way of your own beliefs or opinions?" It would seem there may be many cynics in Church leadership today.

When there is apostasy, deception and heresy in the Church, we cannot turn a blind eye and hope it will just crawl quietly back out of the door through which it entered. We must sound the siren so that church leaders and their flock can come to their senses (see Luke Chapter 15). If church leaders won't wake up, then the sheep need to have the courage to confront Satan's lies with God's Word in the same way that Jesus did when Satan was twisting the Word of God in his attempt to 'persuade' Jesus to obey and worship him. What was Jesus' response to Satan's deceptions?

Jesus said, **"It is written..."** (see Matthew 4:4,7,10 & Luke 4:4,8).

In order to counter Satan's lies, we need to know what is written in God's Word. With all kinds of sexual immorality now being either openly regarded as acceptable in the Church, or being indulged in secretly behind closed doors, or 'hidden' on computers in our homes, we must purposefully remove the veil that has been covering our eyes, and put aside every belief or opinion we hold concerning this subject, especially where our thinking is contrary to God's Word.

Fornication, adultery, masturbation, pornography, homosexuality, lesbianism, bisexuality, transgenderism and other variations of sexuality, are running rampant in the Church, and it seems that very few are prepared to confront and deal with it. In his book, *The Christian Book for Men – Biblical Solutions to the Battles Facing Men*, Chris has talked about aspects of this subject in detail in Chapter Four of Volume One.

Institutional sex abuse scandals in the Church

Over the years, it has been brought to the attention of the world, through the media, that many denominations of the worldwide Church have been involved in wide-scale sexual abuse over many decades, about which they have kept quiet. Many of these incidents have been known about by those as high up the Church ladder as the Archbishops, yet these dark secrets have remained covered up in the hope that they will somehow be forgotten. They are never forgotten by those who have been subjected to the abuse, and many courageous victims have come forward to expose this hidden wickedness. With every new case coming to light, it becomes more and more shocking that this is happening **within** the Church; the place where sinners are supposed to come to confess and repent of their sins, receive God's forgiveness, and be set free from their besetting vices, **not** use the cover of the Church to practice all manner of sin for personal secret gratification, whilst manipulating victims into silence. God sees all this, and He will continue to expose every sin that is being perpetrated by those who are responsible for the flock.

Sexuality and confusion

We have read articles about transgender pastors stating openly that 'God is transgender'. Each month, and sometimes on a weekly basis, we hear of homosexual, lesbian, bisexual and transgender people being appointed into leadership positions in the Church: curates, rectors, vicars, deans, deacons, archdeacons, bishops, as well as other less prominent leadership roles.

Recently, available to read on social media, is the situation of a Church of England school inviting a group called *Mermaids* to teach transgender training to the school staff, resulting in the vicar handing in his resignation as a governor. It was reported that the vicar, The Reverend John Parker, said,

'I was basically told by my bishop...that if I wished to faithfully

follow the Bible then I was no longer welcome in the Church. I felt very much like the Church and the school were silencing me.' [2]

Yes, this sort of thing is happening in a **Church school**! It is highly likely that more incidents like this will occur as time goes on. For more information concerning this story, please see the article on the *Christian Concern* website https://www.christianconcern.com/our-issues/church-and-state/a-bishop-a-vicar-and-mermaids-whos-misleading-whom

And for further details on the ideology and agenda of the *Mermaids* organisation, visit their website www.mermaidsuk.org.uk

To get to the root of this confusion, we need to go right back to the beginning, when God created the human race: He created them male and female (see Genesis 1:27). And just to confirm this fact even more, Jesus Himself said,

"Haven't you read the Scriptures?" Jesus replied. "They record that from the beginning 'God made them male and female.'" – Matthew 19:4

God was not confused when He created the human race. He knew what He wanted to create, and He said that what He created was good (see Genesis 1:31). He created the man first and then the woman (see Genesis 2:15-22). This was the original perfection of the human race when God brought it into being in the Garden of Eden. Adam knew he was a man, and also knew that Eve was a woman (see Genesis 2:22-24). But let us never forget that the moment they disobeyed God's command to not eat of the fruit of the tree of the knowledge of good and evil, sin entered into the very core of their being, and they began to have the knowledge of evil. Their original sin has resulted in all humanity being born with the inherent disposition of sin in our DNA which is loaded in the direction of being persuaded to listen to, believe and follow the lies of the one who is evil; Satan. Most people don't realise that it is Satan who is doing this to their minds. In a very simplified explanation, they will look at their bodies, and something in them will tell them that they are not what they 'should' be. The longer these thoughts are played out in their minds, the more entrenched this belief becomes, until they are so consumed with these thoughts, they cannot live their life unless they do something to change the way they were created. Wanting to change our gender and our identity is basically telling God that He made a mistake when He created us in the gender that we can no longer accept.

A man wants to become a woman, and desires to change his physical appearance to look and feel like a woman, including wearing women's clothing. A woman wants to become a man, and desires to change her physical appearance to look and feel like a man, including wearing men's clothing. Some people want to be non-binary, being neither exclusively male nor female, and fashion designers have jumped onto this bandwagon, creating new lines of 'gender-neutral' clothing. Some want to be bi-sexual, with an attraction to having sexual relationships with either gender.

A Biological Fact

The fact that it is **God** who creates both the sperm of the man and the egg of the woman which are needed to create each human being means that every person on this earth is born either male or female. We cannot get away from this biological **fact**. Our chromosomes and our genitalia determine our physical gender. Faced with this inescapable fact, when a man or woman, a boy or girl look at themselves and dislike or even detest what they see and cannot accept the gender that they biologically are, but want to be the opposite, as hard as it is to accept, they are rebelling against what God created them to be.

We realise that there are some rare cases where, due to a genetic anomaly, a baby may have both male and female genitalia, and those responsible for the child have to make a difficult decision as to which gender the child should be so that the surgery can be undertaken. Or a male child could be born without his genitals (biblically known as a eunuch. See Matthew 19:12 AMP). This is a vastly different situation to what we are seeing today following the flood of promotion of transgender ideology and teaching in our schools, which tells our little primary school age children that they can be whatever gender they want to be, even informing them that they can have surgery and medication to alter their body parts. We read that in California, schools want to teach young children that there are now fifteen different genders to choose from! You can read an article on this by visiting https://www.christianheadlines.com/contributors/michael-foust/california-may-teach-kindergarteners-there-are-15-genders.html

Whatever you may think about this, as of the time of writing, we have read on social media that the BBC are promoting film resources for school children aged 9-12 years, teaching them that there are over 100 gender identities. You can read this information at https://www.christian.org.uk/news/bbc-tells-kids-there-are-more-than-100-gender-identities/

Is it any wonder that we are reading harrowing stories of children who are coming home from school in confusion and distress after listening to teachers telling them that girls are not real, and boys are not real. Even as recently as ten years ago, this kind of teaching was unheard of, and those in positions of care for children would have put in place all manner of measures to protect them from any kind of physical sexual abuse. But it appears that those in authority have completely overlooked or ignored the obvious fact that sexual abuse can be aimed at our minds, causing doubts and confusion particularly in vulnerable young children. Those involved in transgender ideology have grabbed onto this and our schools are now opening their doors and welcoming them in to 'educate' the minds of our children with their twisted beliefs under the guise of what is known in UK schools as 'Sex and Relationship Education'. On their website, the strapline for the *Mermaids* logo is, 'Embrace. Empower. Educate'. This says it all; their policy is to 'educate' and 'train' school staff to get on board with their programme of indoctrinating the minds of every child, thereby placing a seed of doubt in their tender minds causing them to question their identity and to pursue 'different genders' if they desire.

We would encourage you to read the article by *Christian Concern* about the case of The Reverend John Parker. Their article has a link to a disturbing audio of the transgender training session. It should cause us all great concern, and to lobby Government to put a stop to this form of sexual abuse.

Their article can be found by using this link:

https://www.christianconcern.com/our-issues/education/vicar-resigns-after-being-silenced-over-trans-ideology-concerns-at-church-prima

The frightening thing is that several Church denominations are in favour of this education and are actively supporting it. With support from the Archbishop of Canterbury, every bishop would feel compelled to follow suit or be faced with the prospect of losing their job. The bishops would then expect their subordinates to accept this policy, and if any clergy oppose it, they could easily lose their jobs too, as we have seen in the above example of The Reverend John Parker.

So, how is it that a whole Church denomination can endorse and support beliefs and teachings that are diametrically opposed to God's Word? The simple answer is that many of the most senior of Church hierarchy have listened to people who do not know God, who do not love God and do not worship God; people who are atheists, humanists, secularists, and possibly even Satanists. The most senior of Church leaders have made the decision that because 'God is love', then the only thing the Church should do is love everyone by affirming their right to choose what they want to be and what they want to do, under the new Church principle of Mutual Flourishing, which we will look at in Section B.

Basically, the Church is endorsing and supporting rebellion, and shows no sign of intending to challenge it with biblical truth. If our leaders were truly God's watchmen and faithful shepherds of the flock, they would be confronting this deception head on, like Jesus did to Satan, with the words, **"It is written..."**.

So, let's look at a couple of Scriptures relating to God's creation of human beings in the womb:

"You guided my conception and formed me in the womb. You clothed me with skin and flesh, and you knit my bones and sinews together." – Job 10:10-11

"You made all the delicate, inner parts of my body and knit me together in my mother's womb. Thank you for making me so wonderfully complex! Your workmanship is marvelous—how well I know it. You watched me as I was being formed in utter seclusion, as I was woven together in the dark of the womb. You saw me before I was born. Every day of my life was recorded in your book. Every moment was laid out before a single day had passed. How precious are your thoughts about me, O God. They cannot be numbered" – Psalm 139:13-17

Concerning those who question or resent their birth gender, the Word of God says,

"Who are you, a mere human being, to argue with God? Should the thing that was created say to the one who created it, "Why have you made me like this?" – Romans 9:20

With regards to wearing clothes of the opposite sex, God says,

"A woman shall not wear a man's clothing, nor shall a man put on a woman's clothing; for whoever does these things is utterly repulsive to the LORD your God." – Deuteronomy 22:5 AMP

A simple understanding of this Scripture is that a woman is not to dress to try to look like a man, and a man is not to dress to try to look like a woman. God is saying that having a desire or a craving to dress so that we look like the opposite sex is repulsive to Him. He is not being mean by such a statement; He created us and knows what is best for us. Therefore, desiring to be the opposite of the gender we were born with is actually sinful to God.

A man and a woman could both wear shorts and a t-shirt, but in such cases, they are not trying to be opposite to the gender that they actually are. They are simply both wearing clothes that both sexes can wear. Some churches have an issue with women wearing trousers, making false claims that this indicates that a woman is 'dressing as a man'. They go so far as to make it a church rule that women must wear skirts or a dress.

This is not what Deuteronomy 22:5 is saying. The issue is the **motives and intentions in our heart**. Are we purposefully wanting to look and feel like the opposite sex? In the case of women wearing trousers, are women merely wearing a style of clothes that both sexes can wear, with no intention or desire to 'be a man'? Women's fashion trousers are designed to look feminine and in the majority of cases, most women wear trousers for practical reasons such as for warmth and comfort; most have no motive or intention to cross-dress and appear as though they are a man. Also, many women work in an environment where trousers or suits must be worn for corporate appearance. In their outfits, they are still women, and no one looking at them would consider them to be trying to look like a man simply because the outfit includes trousers.

I am sure that many of us have come across someone who is purposefully trying to appear as the opposite of their birth gender. It is obvious even at a first glance. Our minds will immediately confirm to us that what we are seeing is a person trying to be the opposite sex.

Clothing worn in biblical times did not reflect how we dress today. On a website, we read the following concerning clothing worn during that era and how it can still apply today without it suggesting or implying that cross-dressing is occurring:

'We should recall, however, that in biblical times, clothing for males and females was different only in ***styles*** *and* ***details****, not in* ***kind****. Men did not wear trousers and women did not adorn themselves with skirts and blouses. While it undoubtedly is true that God wants some sexual distinction apparent in men's and women's garments, it is not legitimate to say that all women's pants are wrong or, for that matter, that Scottish kilts are sinful for the men of that culture. A woman can be feminine in a* ***modest*** *pant-suit (cf. 1 Tim. 2:9-10) and men can still be masculine in a robe-like garment as in some Near Eastern countries today.'* – www.christiancourier.com (website's own emphasis)

Also, a fascinating read on the historical issue of Deuteronomy 22:5 can be found on the following website;

http://studyholiness.com/doc/What_Deuteronomy_22_5_Really_Means.pdf

As we have mentioned, the issue of questioning our created gender and wanting to change it seems to be a matter of what is going on in the heart. Changing our gender and identity is not really the solution. We have read of many who, after years of having transgendered, have not found it to bring the peace and happiness that they had hoped for. You can find such stories by doing a quick Internet search. Many have discovered that it has brought them more sorrow and wish that they could now revert back to the gender that they were born with. Once gender surgery has been performed and years of hormone treatment has taken its toll, it is impossible to undo the damage that has been done. Yet organisations such as *Mermaids* want to indoctrinate our children with these dangerous thoughts. If a child questions their identity or gender, the parents are not allowed to challenge it; they are instructed that they must support their child's desire to express themselves as a different gender. If they fail to support their child's wishes, they have the threat hanging over them that they may be viewed as incompetent parents and could end up having their child taken away from them.

With this whole issue, society has clearly opened up a can of worms that is uncontainable. What is needed is for God to do a supernatural 'heart surgery' on all who are troubled by this distressing situation. God can change what is going on in our hearts and our minds, transforming everything that is contrary to His Word. Our part is to read His Word, believe His Word and obey His Word. When we know the truth about how He created us, and that He knew who we were whilst we were still in our mother's womb, this truth has the power to heal all the turmoil in our souls concerning our identity. When we know the truth, the truth shall set us free (see John 8:32).

Same-sex relationships & same-sex 'marriage'

We have read of **ordained** ministers in high positions who were previously heterosexually married but have left these God-ordained marriages to pursue relationships with a same-sex partner, claiming that God approves of this new arrangement. We will show clearly that such appointments are contrary to God's Word, and that He is **not** okay with what is going on in His Church, especially when bishops and others in leadership are imparting God's 'blessing' upon the unbiblical lifestyles of such individuals.

So, let us read what is written. As hard as this may be to accept, what God's Word says is written out of His heart of love for us, and for our eternal destiny. Whilst we are saved by grace and not by works, we are also required to live a holy life in obedience to Gods' Word, and not give ourselves over to sinful thoughts and practices. As we will read in some of the following Scriptures, those who carry on in their sinful lives **will not** inherit the kingdom of God. This means that the fires of hell will await their arrival. This really ought to cause great alarm to every professing believer who thinks they can mess around in habitual sin and hope to get away with it.

"So God created man in His own image; in the image of God He created him; male and female He created them." – Genesis 1:27 NKJV

"Then the LORD God said, "It is not good for the man to be alone. I will make a helper who is just right for him." So the LORD God formed from the ground all the wild animals and all the birds of the sky. He brought them to the man to see what he would call them, and the man chose a name for each one. He gave names to all the livestock, all the birds of the sky, and all the wild animals. But still there was no helper just right for him. So the LORD God caused the man to fall into a deep sleep. While the man slept, the LORD God took out one of the man's ribs and closed up the opening. Then the LORD God made a woman from the rib, and he brought her to the man.

"At last!" the man exclaimed. "This one is bone from my bone, and flesh from my flesh! She will be called 'woman,' because she was taken from 'man.'" This explains why a man leaves his father and mother and is joined to his wife, and the two are united into one." – Genesis 2:18-24

"Do not practice homosexuality, having sex with another man as with a woman. It is a detestable sin." – Leviticus 18:22

The Amplified Bible puts that verse like this:

"You shall not lie [intimately] with a male as one lies with a female; it is repulsive."

"If a man practices homosexuality, having sex with another man as with a woman, both men have committed a detestable act;"– Leviticus 20:13(a)

The Amplified Bible puts that verse as follows:

"If a man lies [intimately] with a male as if he were a woman, both men have committed a detestable (perverse, unnatural) act;"

"Don't you realize that those who do wrong will not inherit the Kingdom of God?** Don't fool yourselves. Those who indulge in sexual sin, or who worship idols, or commit adultery, or are male prostitutes, or practice homosexuality, or are thieves, or greedy people, or drunkards, or are abusive, or cheat people — **none of these will

inherit the Kingdom of God." – 1 Corinthians 6: 9-10 (Authors' emphasis)

"For the law was not intended for people who do what is right. It is for people who are lawless and rebellious, who are ungodly and sinful, who consider nothing sacred and defile what is holy, who kill their father or mother or commit other murders. The law is for people who are sexually immoral, or who practice homosexuality, or are slave traders, liars, promise breakers, or who do anything else that contradicts the wholesome teaching that comes from the glorious Good News entrusted to me by our blessed God." – 1 Timothy 1:9-11

"Run away from sexual immorality [in any form, whether thought or behavior, whether visual or written]. Every other sin that a man commits is outside the body, but the one who is sexually immoral sins against his own body. Do you not know that your body is a temple of the Holy Spirit who is within you, whom you have [received as a gift] from God, and that you are not your own [property]? You were bought with a price [you were actually purchased with the precious blood of Jesus and made His own]. So then, honor and glorify God with your body." – 1 Corinthians 6:18-20 AMP

"But sexual immorality and all [moral] impurity [indecent, offensive behavior] or greed must not even be hinted at among you, as is proper among saints [for as believers our way of life, whether in public or in private, reflects the validity of our faith]." – Ephesians 5:3 AMP

"And angels who did not keep their own designated place of power, but abandoned their proper dwelling place, [these] He has kept in eternal chains under [the thick gloom of utter] darkness for the judgment of the great day, just as Sodom and Gomorrah and the adjacent cities, ***since they in the same way as these angels indulged in gross immoral freedom and unnatural vice and sensual perversity. They are exhibited [in plain sight] as an example in undergoing the punishment of everlasting fire."*** – Jude 6-7 AMP (Authors' emphasis)

"But as for you, beloved, remember the [prophetic] words spoken by the apostles of our Lord Jesus Christ. They used to say to you, "In the last days there will be scoffers, following after their own ungodly passions." These are the ones who are [agitators] causing divisions— worldly-minded [secular, unspiritual, ***carnal, merely sensual— unsaved****], devoid of the Spirit."* - Jude 17-19 AMP (Authors' emphasis)

May we also encourage you to read Romans 1:18-27 NLT, 1 Corinthians 6:12-13 AMP and 2 Corinthians 12:20 – 13:5 AMP.

The above Scriptures are just a few of the many passages of God's Holy Word on this subject. This is the Word of the Lord, despite how each of us may personally feel about it. It is God's holy Law. Many of our traditional national laws are based on holy Law, but we are now witnessing the rise of those who are determined to overturn and re-write our traditional laws, relentlessly pushing for Government to implement what they demand in the name of 'equality'. Whether or not our national leaders agree with the cultural climate of our times, it would seem that new laws are being made on the basis of, and to appease, the cries of political correctness. This secular push for change began in the 1960's with the feminist movement, and concerning this movement, Hill says,

'The feminist movement, which is usually defined as a movement for social, economic and political equality of men and women, also involved the rights of women over their own bodies and the recognition that their sexual participation should not be primarily aimed at giving pleasure to men. This sexual freedom helped to encourage the LGBTQ+ movement of sexual libertarianism that grew out of the Gay Pride Movement. The social significance of this movement can hardly be exaggerated. From the beginning, their stated objectives in the 1972 manifesto in Britain, was the destruction of the traditional family, which they said was the 'source of our oppression'.' [3]

In the 1970's, this began to make its way into the Church, but it has now reached the point where it is completely taking over the foundations, principles and teachings of Christianity, with many leaders caving into the pressure to conform to their ways and beliefs. The ways of the world are not God's ways. Jesus says the prince of this world is Satan, the devil. When the Church affirms the ways of the world and incorporates its twisted practices into the very fabric of Christianity, it is essentially bowing down and serving Satan. Once the laws of the land (based on God's holy Laws) are overturned, and what is unlawful now becomes 'legal', we have opened up the floodgates, with no way of reversing it without anarchy breaking out. Once Governments forsake long-held biblical laws and give groups of people what they perceive is their 'legal right', they will never let Government retract their rights without a huge uprising.

Having remained strong for so long on the issue of marriage being between a biological man and a biological woman, many denominations of the Church now seem to feel that they must follow suit and 'normalize' within the Church lifestyles and practices that have always been unlawful in the land up until recent years. Society and the culture of our times may have succeeded in making 'legal' the things that are inherently unlawful in accordance with God's Word, but their 'success' does not overturn His law. So, to keep up with the world, the Church is now discarding God's Word and is accepting 'same-sex marriage' between members of its congregations. Having crossed this line, they are now welcoming and celebrating it amongst the clergy, proudly displaying in Church magazines and on social media, the joy they feel in having succeeded in overturning the Word of God on one of the most holiest of issues.

Unrepentant sexual immorality

As Christians, we have been called to live a holy life (see 2 Peter 2:21). With this knowledge, how can unashamedly promoting a deliberate choice to rebel against this command, and remaining in our sin, ever be an option that we would even consider, let alone actively pursue? What do we think living a holy life actually means if we believe that blatant rebellion against God's Word and proudly living a sinful life is now perfectly acceptable? Expecting other believers to accept our unrepentant lifestyle, and even proactively doing all that we can to change the whole nature and foundation of Christianity to enable us to continue in our chosen way of life, further compounds our sin. No matter how 'Christian' we may outwardly appear to others with our social justice projects and our charitable deeds, we can be sure that, like Judas Iscariot, the devil has entered us, sin has mastered us, and unless we repent, sudden destruction will befall us with catastrophic eternal consequences.

"Whoever remains stiff-necked after many rebukes will suddenly be destroyed—without remedy." – Proverbs 29:1 NIV

Particularly concerning those who govern the Anglican Church, Hill pinpoints the very root of all that we are seeing today in both the world and the Church itself;

'...the drive to maintain unity at all costs – to accommodate all theological beliefs, however contradictory. This is the central weakness of the Anglican Church that guarantees its ineffectiveness and its inability to offer any biblically-based moral, spiritual or social leadership in the nation.' [4]

Further, Hill says,

'This is the tragedy of the church today. The church wants to be like the world so that the world likes the church. Archbishop Justin Welby, leader of the established church, has said that he wants the church "to be more inclusive" - which is politically correct code for saying that he wants the church to fall in line with the values of the secular humanist LGBT-friendly society. In other words this is the same spirit as the people who said to Ezekiel, "We want to be like the people of the world who serve wood and stone". So we now have an idolatrous institutional church, an apostate church, a church purporting to be Christian, but with a Christianity without Christ and without a gospel of redemption.' [5]

Let us remember Paul's words of warning to all believers; the shepherds as well as the sheep:

"Do not be deceived and deluded and misled; God will not allow Himself to be sneered at (scorned, disdained, or mocked by mere pretensions or professions, or by His precepts being set aside.) [He inevitably deludes himself who attempts to delude God.] For whatever a man sows, that and that only is what he will reap." – Galatians 6:7 AMPC

This passage uses the word 'precept'. The Cambridge dictionary (www.dictionary.cambridge.org) defines it as *"a rule for action or behaviour, especially obtained from moral thought."* God is saying that we are deceived and deluded if we think that we can mock Him with our pretentious, disdainful professions of faith; sneering, scorning, and setting aside His precepts – His rules for moral action and behaviour.

In spite of the above Scriptures, we have recently discovered that the Christian organisation called 'OneBodyOneFaith' (formerly the Gay Christian Movement) makes the following statement, as part of a fuller statement concerning its company objects:

'It is the conviction of the members of OneBodyOneFaith that human sexuality, sexual orientation and gender identity in all their richness are gifts of God gladly to be accepted, enjoyed and honoured as a way of both expressing and growing in love, in accordance with the life and teaching of Jesus Christ. Therefore it is their conviction that it is entirely compatible with the Christian faith not only to love another person of the same sex, but also to express that love fully in a personal sexual relationship.' [6]

At the time of writing this, the trustees of this organisation include ordained members of the Church of England and the Methodist Church.

The full objects of this organisation can be viewed at:

www.onebodyonefaith.org.uk/about-us/what-we-believe/

By any Spirit-filled believer's understanding of Scripture, this statement is heretical, and is an abandonment of the clearly written Word of God.

In addition to this, today it has been brought to our attention that a 'celebrity pastor' from America, whose views concerning sexual purity are diametrically opposed to the Holy Word of God, has been welcomed by the Church of England. Her teachings against traditional, biblical sexual purity have encouraged many young women, who have made a commitment of 'no sex before marriage', to forsake their pledge and discard their 'purity-rings' which are the symbol of their vow of chastity. This pastor has then melted down all these rings and made the molten metal into a statue of the female genitalia, supposedly as a sign of 'liberating' them from their chastity… and the Church of England has knowledge of this, and appears to have no intention of confronting this outrageous immorality. How far the Church has fallen to find itself at the stage where it sees no problem in welcoming the godless teachings of a pastor who equally sees no problem in proudly leading multitudes of young people into sexual sin.

For more information on this recent incident, we encourage you to read the article which you can find on the following link:

https://anglicanmainstream.org/c-of-e-welcomes-american-celebrity-pastors-attack-on-orthodox-sexual-ethics/

Any belief held by professing Christians, that is contrary to God's Word, is a lie planted in their mind by the antichrist. It would seem that many in the Church have forgotten that God is an all-consuming fire (see Hebrews 12:29).

There are those within the Church who will say that when Jesus first came, He fulfilled the law, and that all Old Testament law has been made void because we now live under grace, and so continuing to engage in sin is not an issue. We do indeed live under God's wonderful grace, but the partial truths of those who make such statements are twisted lies of Satan. The Billy Graham website corrects this lie as follows:

'The moral laws—those against lying, stealing, immorality, etc.—show us how far we fall short of God's will and how badly we need salvation as a free gift, earned by Jesus' death on the cross (Galatians 3:24).

Once we accept God's free gift of eternal life through repentance from sin and faith in Jesus, the moral law becomes a guide for how we live out our new life in Christ by the power of the Holy Spirit (Galatians 5:16-26). The civil laws of Israel have passed away, since the church is not a nation.

The ritual laws of sacrifice, priesthood, and temple have been fulfilled in Jesus, and are no longer applicable to the church (see the book of Hebrews). However, the basic moral law of the Old Testament is clearly reflected in the New Testament guidelines for the Christian life (e.g. Colossians, chapter 3) and is summarized by Jesus in Matthew 22:37-40.' [7]

This can be viewed at www.billygraham.org/answer/which-of-the-hundreds-of-old-testament-laws-are-applicable-to-us-as-christians/

A clear and simple check as to whether an Old Testament law still applies today is to read what the New Testament writers had to say. Paul is very clear about what types of sin will result in a person 'not inheriting the kingdom of God'. We showed you many Scriptures previously, from Paul and other New Testament writers, as well as some spoken by our Saviour Himself.

Furthermore, in the Book of Acts, when the apostles were discussing what the Gentile believers should do, as opposed to what some Jewish believers were trying to force them to fulfil, the apostles replied to them as follows:

*"**Abstain from** things sacrificed to idols, and from [consuming] blood, and from [eating the meat of] things that have been strangled, and **from sexual impurity. If you keep yourselves from these things,***

you will do well." – Acts 15:29 (AMP) (Authors' emphasis)

It is clear that this verse confirms what is written in Leviticus 20:13, that sexual immorality, which includes homosexual and lesbian sex (see Romans 1:26-27 both AMP and NLT) is wrong in the eyes of God under the new covenant of grace, as well as under the old covenant.

We think it would be fair to say that most Christians believe that God's command **to flee from sexual immorality** (in 1 Corinthians 6:18) is solely directed towards those who are actually **committing** this sin. Yes, it is directed to them, but this command to flee must surely **also** apply to all believers who find themselves in a situation where they are under the leadership of those who are openly and unrepentantly committing sexual immorality, and are twisting God's Word in order to teach the flock that this is now acceptable to God.

Let's use our imaginations for a moment. If you were walking down a street and decided to go into a nice shop that you were always familiar with, only to find that it had suddenly been **taken over** and was now an 'adult porn' shop, would you hang around in it? No! You would be horrified and would flee from that place as fast as possible, and never return! You would most likely warn others that this nice shop had been taken over, urging them not to go in there too.

We need to have this same mindset concerning our churches. They may have been lovely, godly churches for decades, and even centuries, but if the demonic has slithered in and seems to be taking over the House of God, we need to get out as fast as we possibly can.

Women in Headship positions in the Church

Michele has written this section, as a Christian woman to other Christian women. It is a difficult issue, but it has been written from her heart, with her primary focus and priority to obey God's Word, even though to do so may result in much resistance.

As we saw in Chapter 1, with the evidence of many Scriptures, God's Word clearly sets out the pattern for those He requires to be in positions of Church leadership. Just to be clear, we are not talking about roles of **ministry** in the Church; yes of course women are to serve and use their giftings in ministry in the Church, in accordance with Scripture, and there are many ways in ministry that women can express their service to God for the benefit of the body of Christ. What we are talking about here is the **headship** and **leadership** of each individual church. Ministry roles can be carried out by both men and women, but God's Word clearly states that the overall headship of every church must be held by a man. God has appointed the man to shepherd the flock and instruct them in the ways of the Lord. Women can assist them in this task, but the man must remain as the head.

In the past twenty years or so, women seem to have taken a dislike to this biblical fact. Disgruntled feminist attitudes have begun to push against God's holy order and have succeeded in getting what they demand. Men in high office have bowed down to the 'I want' cries of many women who are not content to fulfil the biblical roles that God has ordained for them. Let us remember that God created woman to be man's **helper** (see Genesis 2:18-21) not to be the head of the man. As much as many of today's Church women don't like it, there is no getting away from the fact that Scripture clearly states that the husband is the head of the wife (see Ephesians 5:23), and so it is that God has appointed that men be in headship of the Church. Without a doubt, the 'rebellion of Eve' is very much alive and kicking in the Church; the original rebellion that questions, "Did God **really** say…?" It is a question that says, "I don't like what God has said, so I am going to do something about it. I am going to push and protest until I can get what I want." It is rooted in an apparent 'injustice', causing a feeling that a 'wrong' has been done to women by God Himself. With an attitude of, "How dare God treat women like this!" the first small trickle of 'women's lib' in the Church has now swollen into a raging torrent and is threatening to wash us all away in its wake.

Throughout the Bible, right from the very start in Genesis, we see that God has created everything in an order. When we push to get our own way and go against His order, we end up with confusion and chaos. But not being content to give glory to God as being the helper to God's men, we now have women in leadership roles over men; female priests, vicars, deacons, deans, and even female bishops in authority over all the men below them, which is contrary to God's order for His Church. As women of God, when we die, our obituaries and epitaphs may read of our great earthly achievements, but if they have been gained at the expense of obedience to God's Word, our successes will be blown away like chaff in the wind when we stand before the judgement seat of Christ. The only thing that will determine our eternal destiny will be whether we obeyed God's Word, or rebelled.

Before we move on to the next sub-heading, we wish to make it clear that we recognise that there are women who hold positions such as being a curate or vicar of an individual church and are accountable to the main overseer who is a man. But as we are getting to the stage where almost 25% of UK Anglican bishops are now female (see https://en.wikipedia.org/wiki/List_of_bishops_in_the_Church_of_England), then clearly it is obvious that any local female minister will soon find that their main overseer is not a man. The consequence of this is that when an archbishop appoints a woman into the position of a bishop (the main overseer of a diocese), he has overstepped biblical boundaries and has moved out of God's order of things, resulting in confusion, upset and division. If we would simply obey God's instructions that leaders of churches should be men (who meet the biblical qualification that we set out in Chapter 1), then none of this confusion and upset would occur.

"God is a Female"

With this ascent of female leaders, we are now hearing of

Christian feminists challenging God's Word by stating that God is neither male nor female, citing Galatians 3:28 as their example, but taking it totally out of context and using it as the basis to support their 'claim'. In context with the verse before it, it says,

"And all who have been united with Christ in baptism have put on Christ, like putting on new clothes. There is no longer Jew or Gentile, slave or free, male and female. For you are all one in Christ Jesus." – Galatians 3:27-28

This passage is not even talking about God! It is stating that all who become followers of Christ are no longer seen by God according to all their different nationalities, positions in life, or whether they are born a male or a female; He simply sees each one of us in-Christ. How Christian feminists can take this Scripture and twist it so far out of context to make their claim that God is female, is mind-boggling!

If we were to use that argument to describe God's gender, then we could equally claim that He was a hen, because in Luke 13:34, Jesus said that He longed to gather the people of Jerusalem under His wing as a hen gathers her chicks. Does making such a statement make Jesus a hen? Absolutely not!

Along with all this, some women leaders are attempting to change the wording of long-established liturgy so that God is portrayed in a female manner, with 'new teaching' that God should be referred to in the female form as 'mother God'. They cast aside the truth that Jesus Himself called God His **Father**, and taught us the Lord's Prayer, saying "**Our Father**" and all throughout the Bible, from start to finish, God is called 'Father'. We just did a quick search in the four Gospels alone, and in one translation, over seventy times Jesus refers to God as 'Father', or 'My Father', and **never** as 'mother'. In the Bible, both Jesus and Paul used the word 'Abba' in relation to God (see Mark 14:36, Romans 8:15, Galatians 4:6). Here is the Google definition of the Hebrew meaning of this word:

"A transliteration of the Aramaic term ***abba*** *also appears three*

times in the Greek New Testament of The Bible. Each time the term appears in transliteration it is followed immediately by the translation ho pater in Greek, which literally ***means*** *"the father." In each case it is used with reference to God."*

This seems pretty straightforward and unambiguous! Women leaders may think that their advance up the Church ranks is progress and success for equality for women, but when women go against God's divine and holy order and also outspokenly promote God in a gender that is contrary to what is clearly revealed in His Word, they are actually in rebellion. In God's eyes, rebellion is **not** progress; **it is sin** (see 1 Samuel 15:23).

The whole worldly feminist mindset seems to be the driving force behind women in the Church re-gendering not only God, but in some cases Jesus and the Holy Spirit as well. This worldly passion to push and succeed in getting what they want from the Church, even when the goal they are striving for usurps God's holy instructions, will only reward them with the praises of 'man' for their apparent success in life this side of the grave. All that we build upon the foundation of God, and under the label of Christianity, will be exposed for what it really is on the Day of Judgement. Everything will be judged by God's Word.

"There is a judge for the one who rejects me and does not accept my words; the very words I have spoken will condemn them at the last day." – John 12:48 NIV

If we have built our 'kingdoms' in ways that are diametrically opposed to Scripture, in due time God's Word will beat against our 'kingdoms' and they will crumble like a house built upon the sand (see Matthew 7:24-27). God created order for His own purposes. Even though we may not understand or like His order, it is better for Christian women to obey God's Word and live our lives on earth in the divine order that He created us to live, as man's helper. Disobeying God's order will ultimately reap His judgement, whether that be for the wilful pride of wanting to succeed above men and be in authority over them, or simply accepting a position in the Church that Scripture shows God has not ordained for women to undertake. The following passage is a sober reminder of the place of all humanity in life; what we think, say and do is under the ever-watchful eye of our almighty, powerful God. If this is wise counsel to all humanity, then it most certainly applies to all within the Church:

"When all has been heard, the end of the matter is: fear God [worship Him with awe-filled reverence, knowing that He is almighty God] and keep His commandments, for this applies to every person. For God will bring every act to judgment, every hidden and secret thing, whether it is good or evil." – Ecclesiastes 12:13-14 AMP

God's created order is actually for our good! God is not a woman-hater! He is not being sexist by appointing men to be the head over women. His order is His **will**, and our obedience to it will reap the best for our lives. Without order in life, confusion and chaos is the result. Once these occur, the whole fabric of life crumbles. Rebellion in the Church will result in confusion, chaos, and ultimately collapse.

Chapter 4 - Section B

Mutual Flourishing; The Prosperity 'gospel'; The Social Justice 'gospel'; 'Christian' Entertainment and Social Events - but no preaching; Denial of the Foundations of Christianity

Mutual Flourishing

In 2014 the Church of England introduced a new idea referred to as 'Mutual Flourishing'. Since the idea was originated by the Church of England, we consulted on this subject with The Right Reverend Dr Gavin Ashenden, former Chaplain to Her Majesty the Queen. As such we feel confident to write the following:

The principle of 'mutual flourishing' is the idea that each and every person who enters the Church, and proclaims that they are a follower of Christ, should be given the space and the ability to grow and flourish in whatever way they desire. That sounds good on the surface; of course we are meant to grow in Christ and use the gifts that we have for His glory. The problem arises with what is the intent behind the person's desire to be allowed to mutually flourish. From a biblical perspective, any flourishing must be done **within** the boundaries that God has set in His Holy Word for those in His Church. As we have seen in the previous section, when God's Word says that women have been created to be man's helper, women should not usurp God's divine order on this by pushing for the right to be appointed into positions of high office in the Church which places them in authority over men. Using this tactic to succeed in ministry is far from what could be deemed as 'being allowed to mutually flourish' - it is outright disobedience and rebellion against God's Word.

Also, when God's Word clearly shows in Genesis 2:18-25 that the relationship He has created, ordained and blessed is between a biological male and a biological female (which is established at our conception in our mother's womb), if a man in the Church decides that he wants to be 'married' to a man, or a woman in the Church decides that she wants to be 'married' to a woman, this new concept of mutual flourishing now gives them permission to do so, seemingly without question. Also, when a male believer or a female believer decides that they no longer want to be the gender that God created them to be in their mother's womb, and undergoes treatment and surgery to transition into the gender they now desire to be, mutual flourishing allows them the privacy and the space to do this, without question, so much so that churches are now re-writing baptism liturgy to enable transgendered people to be re-baptised as their new gender.

The Church is also going along with the UK Government's banning of 'gender conversion therapy' and 'homosexual conversion therapy' when in fact the role of the Church is to help those who wish to be set free, when they come to church leaders and openly confess that they are struggling with confusion over their sexuality. God is the only one who can take us as we are, with all our sins, and transform us by the power of the Holy Spirit. The Church is failing the flock drastically when it reneges on its duty to stand up for what God has appointed it to do, and instead bows down to the demands of a political system which wants to dispose of God and the teachings of Christianity in every area of life, including **within** the Church itself. They want the Church to be run on the 'values' of the world's ungodly culture, and those in Church hierarchy appear to be doing nothing to stop it; indeed, liberals and ultraliberals are working hard to encourage it. Referring to the Church in the 1970's, Hill says,

'More than half of the bishops in the Church of England by this time were theological liberals as were many clergy and Free Church ministers.' [8]

Those who are appointed as shepherds over the sheep, who are supposed to be keeping watch over our souls by teaching us to obey the Word of God, now no longer seem to be concerned about what

God has to say. They now want to please the desires of the flock, encouraging and helping them to achieve their personal goals, even if those goals are things which are contrary to God's Word. Mutual flourishing is based on the principle of expressing love to everyone, and this love is demonstrated to them by letting them be and do whatever they want. When those in Church authority give their permission and blessing to the fulfilment of desires and wishes that are contrary to God's Word, the result is that the conscience of those who have received this misguided ecclesiastical blessing is now 'clear'. Their conscience may now be able to feel 'free' in this life, but the Day of Judgement will expose our unrepentant sin and rebellion, and we will not be able to escape it. It will be exposed to us like that of a light from a lighthouse bursting through the dark, thick fog smothering the sea. Our sin **will** be found out at the last day.

The reality is that mutual flourishing is a nice-sounding deception (a lie of Satan) based on the principle that, in the Church, we can be whatever we want, and do whatever we want without anyone challenging us with Jesus' command to repent of our sins (see Matthew 4:17) or obey His Word (see John 3:36; 14:15,21,24; 15:10). Letting people be and do whatever they want, without guidance and godly boundaries, is actually **not** loving at all, as it will eventually reap disaster and all manner of consequences (see Proverbs 14:12).

Liberal progressive Christianity majors on loving everyone as they are, and that there is no need to make anyone feel uncomfortable with teaching that will cause them to be confronted with their sinfulness. But what does God's Word say about love from a biblical sense?

*"And **this is love: that we walk in accordance with His commandments and are guided continually by His precepts.** This is the commandment, just as you have heard from the beginning, that you should [always] walk in love."* – 2 John 6 AMP (Authors' emphasis)

So, authentic Christianity clearly states that biblical love means we live out our Christian life **in accordance with God's commandments and guided continually by God's precepts.** As we have previously seen, 'precepts' means "a rule for action or behaviour, especially obtained from moral thought." So, our outward actions and behaviour are to flow from morally upright thinking. Where do we obtain this moral code of conduct? From God's precepts which are found in His Holy Word. We will not find teaching and guidance in authentic morality anywhere else. The world's 'morality' is nothing but shifting sand, being shaped by the ever-changing tides of secular thinking which wants to remove God from every aspect of life and society.

In order to love others biblically, that will include the tough love of having to draw people aside to talk with them about issues of morality (their sin) and showing them what God's Word says so that they can be brought to a place where they will accept that what they are doing is sinful and will confess and repent of it. The love of God guides, corrects, rebukes, reproves and warns, in order to keep the sheep close to The Shepherd (Jesus), and to stay on the straight and narrow path that leads to eternal life. The following passage of Scripture, of Paul's teaching to Timothy, explains this in the most powerful way:

"I solemnly charge you in the presence of God and of Christ Jesus, who is to judge the living and the dead, and by His appearing and His kingdom: preach the word [as an official messenger]; be ready when the time is right and even when it is not [keep your sense of urgency, whether the opportunity seems favorable or unfavorable, whether convenient or inconvenient, whether welcome or unwelcome]; correct [those who err in doctrine or behavior], warn [those who sin], exhort and encourage [those who are growing toward spiritual maturity], with inexhaustible patience and [faithful] teaching. For the time will come when people will not tolerate sound doctrine and accurate instruction [that challenges them with God's truth]; but wanting to have their ears tickled [with something pleasing], they will accumulate

for themselves [many] teachers [one after another, chosen] to satisfy their own desires and to support the errors they hold,..." – 2 Timothy 4:1-3 AMP

Let us heed where this new teaching of mutual flourishing is leading us and cause us to come before the Lord and repent of chasing after our own ways. The only true flourishing for a follower of Christ is what we call 'Biblical Flourishing', which is based solely on believing God's Word on every matter of life, and then obeying it. Mutual flourishing, as we have seen, allows believers to be and do whatever they want regardless of what God's Word says, and letting believers feel comfortable in continuing in their sins. Mutual flourishing is a heresy which should be abolished. The Church should return to authentic Christianity, with its sole purpose of preaching the uncompromising Word of God; the truth, the whole truth, and nothing but the truth...so help us God.

The Prosperity 'gospel'

The deception of the 'prosperity gospel' is rampant in today's modern church culture, with its message of "send us your best gift and God will bless you and give you wealth, healing, and breakthrough" as well as the life-coaching mantra of "have your best life now!" This is a false gospel based on the love of money and materialism, preying on desperate people and luring them into their lair with its 'promise' of receiving everything that we want in this earthly life. It sounds just like Satan's temptation towards Jesus in the wilderness, promising Jesus that if He worshipped him, he would give Jesus the whole world! (see Luke 4:5-8). This deceptive teaching in the Church does nothing but line the pockets and the lifestyles of those who are peddling it, building their own kingdoms of wealth and affluence, instead of the kingdom of God.

Paul warns Timothy about such people, and exhorts him to flee from this kind of deception:

"But those who [are not financially ethical and] crave to get rich

[with a compulsive, greedy longing for wealth] fall into temptation and a trap and into many foolish and harmful desires that plunge people into ruin and destruction [leading to personal misery]. For the love of money [that is, the greedy desire for it and the willingness to gain it unethically] is a root of all sorts of evil, and some by longing for it have wandered away from the faith and pierced themselves [through and through] with many sorrows. But as for you, O man of God, flee from these things; aim at and pursue righteousness [true goodness, moral conformity to the character of God], godliness [the fear of God], faith, love, steadfastness, and gentleness." – 1 Timothy 6:9-11 AMP

Paul also has a word to say about this to the believers at Corinth:

"For we are not, like so many, [like hucksters making a trade of] peddling God's Word [shortchanging and adulterating the divine message]*; but like [men] of sincerity and the purest motive, as [commissioned and sent] by God, we speak [His message] in Christ (the Messiah), in the [very] sight and presence of God."* – 2 Corinthians 2:17 AMPC (Authors' emphasis)

God's desire is that we prosper **spiritually**. There are some Scriptures that say we will reap what we sow in this life (see Mark 10:29-30), which suggests that we may also prosper in a material and financial sense. However, falling for the manipulation of the prosperity gospel is not the way to go about receiving God's provision. In fact, Jesus teaches that we should sell all we have and give it to the poor (see Matthew 19:21-22). This is in stark contrast to the obscenely affluent lifestyles of some high-profile 'celebrity' Christian leaders.

If God does prosper us abundantly, both materially and financially, that is a wonderful blessing, but we are not to horde it to ourselves with a proud attitude that says, "Look at me! Look at all that I have got! God must think I am really great to give me all this prosperity and success!"

When we are blessed with God's abundance, we are exhorted to sow it back into His kingdom by giving to those who are struggling and oppressed, helping the poor, the widows and the orphans. Society is awash with the evidence of poverty and injustice, so there are plenty of things that we could sow our abundance into for God's glory, rather than believing it is okay to buy ourselves the latest £250,000 car, multimillion-dollar private jet or luxury mansion.

Do not be sucked into the kind of 'Christianity' which majors on promoting and preaching the prosperity gospel. Check your Bible to see whether or not what is being taught lines up with Scripture. If it doesn't, then obey what Jesus says, not what these imposters proclaim under the banner of 'Christianity'.

The Social Justice 'gospel'; 'Christian' Entertainment and Social Events – but no preaching

The ethos behind this recent movement in the Christian arena is, "Let's do the work and meet the needs of our communities, but we won't preach about Jesus. We will just 'be Jesus' to the people, so that they can see God's love for them. We can simply 'love them into the kingdom.'" At first glance, this looks like a lovely non-threatening way to go about our Christian witness. But this is actually contrary to God's Word.

Concerning people who have not heard about Jesus Christ, the apostle Paul says,

*"For everyone who calls upon the name of the Lord [invoking Him as Lord] will be saved. But how are people to call upon Him Whom they have not believed [in Whom they have no faith, on Whom they have no reliance]? **And how are they to believe in Him [adhere to, trust in, and rely upon Him] of Whom they have never heard? And how are they to hear without a preacher?** And how can men [be expected to] preach unless they are sent?"* – Romans 10:13-15(a) AMPC (Authors' emphasis)

Clearly, we are meant to speak about Jesus, not just do 'good works' in our communities and the wider world. Many churches have opened their doors as a 'marketplace' to raise funds for the church building, or other projects. More people seem to come to church buildings to get involved in whatever the church may be hosting, rather than to hear the Gospel; events such as flower festivals, craft fairs, Christmas tree festivals, May Day festivals, fashion shows, jigsaw puzzle festivals, non-Christian concerts, and recently we came across an advert outside a church which was holding a balloon festival!

We have heard of churches hosting 'film nights', showing films that are 'family-friendly' but are non-Christian. This can attract a lot of people from the community, and it all sounds very harmless, and in itself is a way to welcome people who wouldn't normally cross the threshold into a church. But unless we are doing something at these events to at least inform people about Jesus Christ and salvation through faith in Him, then all these people will go home none the wiser that they are still on the wide path that leads to hell. It would be better to encourage our local community halls to host such non-Christian events than to encourage people to come into our church building, using a film night as an 'evangelism tool', but never actually telling anyone what they must do to be saved. If we do feel that we want to host film nights, then there are plenty of good Christian based films available that we could show which may sow a seed in the hearts of all those attending. But a word of caution: discernment is needed when selecting even Christian-based films, as some blockbuster Christian films send a message that is devoid of repentance, giving a subtle suggestion that all humanity will be saved, regardless of whether we believe in Jesus or not. When we, as churches, do all these non-preaching activities under the banner of 'Christianity', what exactly are we doing, and what are we hoping to achieve?!

Besides these pleasant social events designed to attract our communities, churches are also letting organisations use their premises for a whole host of social and community activities, some of which ought never to be occurring in the House of God, because of their pagan origins. But many church leaders now seem to have second thoughts about turning away the income of certain kinds of unbiblical business for fear of being hauled into court for 'discrimination'.

Over the past 5 years or so, we have cast a regular glance at the many activities that take place in church buildings. Many of these are spiritually desecrating the House of God. This reminds us of when Jesus entered the Temple and saw people 'doing business'. He became really angry - with a righteous anger - that the people were misusing the holy place.

"And Jesus went into the temple (whole temple enclosure) and drove out all who bought and sold in the sacred place, and He turned over the four-footed tables of the money changers and the chairs of those who sold doves. He said to them, The Scripture says, My house shall be called a house of prayer; but you have made it a den of robbers." – Matthew 21:12-13 AMPC

Again, it needs to be asked; when we allow other people to use our church buildings, are we sharing the Gospel with them when they come in, or are we just letting them use the House of God for their community activities? It seems that church leaders would prefer to be seen to be reaching out to the community to 'please man' by meeting the social needs, rather than please God by preaching the Gospel message of forgiveness of sins and salvation through faith in Jesus Christ. People's souls will not be saved from hell just because we let the community use the House of God for their activities.

Yes, we do need to do these good works, but not to the exclusion of preaching the Gospel message. We need to deliver the message and do the deeds. When we run a soup kitchen for the homeless and those in poverty, we need to give them the Bread of Life (the Word of God) to save their souls from eternity in hell, as well as give them actual bread to save them from starvation.

We realise that many will misunderstand us, or even feel quite hostile to what we have just written. We are fully aware that any number of Scriptures could be quoted to us seemingly accusing us of the very issues we are trying to address in this work – apostasy, deception and heresy; all lies of Satan. One Scripture that comes to mind which people could use against us is, ***"Pure and genuine religion in the sight of God the Father means caring for orphans and widows in their distress*** *and refusing to let the world corrupt you."* – James 1:27(a) (Authors' emphasis)

The point we are wishing to make here is perhaps best summed up as follows: God, indeed, is desperate for us to love our neighbour (all people) with His agape love. He is crying out for us to help those in need and to go the extra mile, even for strangers, as the Good Samaritan did. **But** if we do not believe the unsaved are going to spend eternity in hell, then we will not understand that social action **alone** will save nobody. At best it will only help people get through the crises of this temporal life. Jesus told His disciples that the poor will be with us **always** (see John 12:1-8) and His final command was that we go and make disciples, baptising them and **teaching them** to **obey His commands** (see Matthew 28:16-20). Therefore, it is essential that whatever social action we take under the banner of Christianity must include the preaching of the Gospel so that people can know what they must do to be saved and be assured of their salvation when they die. When the Church fails to do this, it is failing in the whole purpose for which God created it. It is no good only helping to save someone's earthly life, if their soul is still headed for hell when they die.

Loving people is biblical, but the phrase 'loving them into the kingdom' is not! The Church is to love the unsaved, preach the Gospel to them and baptise and make disciples of those who wish to follow Jesus, and then teach them to obey His Word. **That** is the way that Jesus has set things out. Anything other than what Jesus has clearly told us to do will lead many to believe that they are saved when, in reality, they are not. Do Church leaders really want that responsibility on their heads on the Day of Judgement?

It is interesting that the **last part** of the verse above, which we have highlighted here, says, *"Pure and genuine religion in the sight of God the Father means...* ***refusing to let the world corrupt you.****"* (Authors' emphasis). This is our whole point; the Church today is allowing itself to be corrupted by the ways and the mindset of the world, and is failing to preach and hold up the Word of God against the flood of cultural and social agendas that are crashing against its doors.

Denial of the Foundations of Christianity

It is hard to believe that people who profess to be mature, born again believers could deny any of God's Word, but we have come across some in leadership (and in the pews) who have expressed a negative or disbelieving view of many of the things we have listed below. There are some in leadership who do not believe the Bible at all! Having said this, we need to share with you that, in order for what we have written here to be accepted as fact, the Holy Spirit will need to have convicted you that God's written Word (The Holy Bible) is absolute truth. For the first twenty years of my (Chris) Christian life, I did not believe that the Bible was absolute truth. I was a nominal believer, merely going through the outward religious motions of Christianity. But once I became born again and Spirit-filled in 1991, what follows in this section began to make sense to me. I did not have to try to make sense of it; the Holy Spirit in me enabled me to understand the Word of God.

In some of the sub-headings below we have given you the Scripture references so you can check them out for yourself. In other sections we have written more extensively and have included the actual Scripture passages.

Creation

We have heard members of clergy firmly state that they don't take the biblical account of God creating the heavens and the earth (and everything in them) literally. In fact some have stated that the 'Big Bang' theory, together with our evolving out of some big pot of slime is a more 'realistic' scenario to them! Let's put it this way; what is the probability of an explosion in a scrap metal yard resulting in all the metal pieces coming together to produce a top of the range Ferrari?! Zero! Yet this is what they want us to believe when they deny creation according to God's Word. For God's incredible account of Creation, read Genesis Chapters 1 and 2.

The Fall

We have heard people say that they think the story of Adam and Eve in the Garden of Eden (their being enticed to sin against God's command to not eat the forbidden fruit, and their being banished from the Garden) is just some fairy story and not something that really happened. God's Word tells us that it did happen, and all humanity that has been born since that time is the result of that incident. For God's account of The Fall of man, read Genesis Chapter 3. Without understanding the truth of where sin originates from, the whole purpose of Christianity, including spiritual warfare against the daily onslaughts of Satan and his demons, will make no sense.

The Virgin Birth

We have read about, and heard with our own ears, members of clergy mock the truth of the virgin birth. God Himself chose Mary, and He sent the angel Gabriel to her personally to inform her that she was highly favoured by God, and that she would be the mother of Jesus, the Son of God. Those who deny this are demonstrating a serious defiance against God. For the Word of God on this sacred and holy truth, read Matthew Chapter 1, and Luke Chapters 1 and 2.

The Trinity

High up in the corridors of Church authority, certain figures are debating the removal of the Trinity from Church doctrine. The argument for this is mainly that the word 'Trinity' does not appear in the Bible. That word itself may not be in the Bible, but the three persons of the Trinity most definitely are! The Father, the Son and the Holy Spirit are the Holy Trinity, and to remove the word from our speech and our sermons is to remove the entire Godhead from Christianity. If we remove the Father, Son and Holy Spirit, then we are removing all that our Christian faith stands on. Without the Trinity there is no Christianity.

See Matthew 28:19 for biblical evidence of the three persons of the Trinity, which are Jesus's own Words. In the very beginning (see Genesis 1:26), God said, "Let **us** make…". The word 'us' indicates that there is more than one person. We are not called to understand the concept of the Trinity; we are simply called to believe it.

The Cross, the Resurrection and the Ascension

It seems beyond comprehension that Christians would deny any of these facts about Jesus, but shockingly many do. In recent times, we have read about and also heard of leaders of high position in the Church who deny all or some of these. They quite strongly state that Jesus did not die on the cross, that He did not rise from the dead and that He did not ascend into heaven. If this is what they believe, why are they calling themselves a Christian, and even more importantly, what exactly are they doing working in the Church when they do not believe these vital facts? God's truth on these founding truths of Christianity can be read in Matthew Chapters 26, 27, 28 and Acts Chapter 1, and throughout the New Testament. Liberal Theology, which questions many of the foundational truths of Christianity, is **unbelief**, and it originates from the devil.

We are Sinners

Some do not believe that we are sinners in need of salvation. They believe that we are all born with a good heart and with a desire to do good, and that God is okay with our natural failings. In contrast to such liberal thinking, the Bible says we have all sinned and continually fall short of His glory (see Romans 3:23). The Bible says that foolishness is bound up in the heart of children and the rod of correction (correction given with godly wisdom and loving-kindness) is needed to drive it far from them (see Proverbs 22:15). A child that is not given godly correction and is left to itself brings shame (see Proverbs 29:15). Clearly, we are all born with the inherent disposition of sin, since The Fall of Adam and Eve. The disposition to sin is hard-wired into our DNA. Newborn babies look pure and innocent at first, but soon after their first birthday they begin to show their wilfulness to be naughty. No one has taught them how to be naughty; they just seem to know that rebelling against obeying their parents is something that they can try to do! God created human beings, and He says that we are sinners and need to be saved (see Matthew 1:21).

Confession and Repentance of Sin

Many progressive and liberal churches preach that, once we have given our lives to Christ, we don't need to confess and repent of our daily sins anymore. This kind of preaching tells its hearers that if we sin, we can just forget about it and get on with life, because God loves us and forgives us, so our sin doesn't matter anymore. They preach that it is okay for us to remain the way we are, and that obeying God's Word on repentance is now 'optional'. This is a deceptive teaching that says, "You repented once at the start, when you gave your life to Christ, so that covers you for everything; so when you sin, don't worry about it."

Many churches are failing to preach that we must crucify our flesh (see Galatians 5:24) and that we must **sin no more** (see John 8:11). This latter Scripture is a **command** of Jesus, not an optional extra!

Even more shockingly, we are living in a time where many leaders are actually saying that we don't need to repent **at all**! Their basis for Christianity is that God's grace covers all our sins, and as such, we don't need to deal with our sins; we simply need to love each other. They have taken just one of Jesus' teachings, to "love our neighbour as ourselves", and thrown out the rest of His teachings, that we must repent of our sin, be born again, and obey His Word. We think the only explanation for this is that such people cannot truly be born again. The simple truth is that we cannot stop sinning unless we **are** born again and filled with the Holy Spirit. We cannot stop sinning unless we crucify the cravings of our natural flesh. Once we are born again, we realise that we are saved by God's grace alone, and knowing that truth, encourages us to not want to grieve our heavenly Father by rebelling against His Holy Word, which in essence is what sin is; rebellion and ignorance. Sin believes the lie that says, "I am in a better place to know what is right for me, more than anyone else, and that includes God." Many of today's Christians want to be welcomed but not warned, affirmed but not affected, comforted but not convicted, and saved but not sanctified.

Michele has dialogued with Christians on social media, some whose profiles indicate that they are members of clergy, who, when she has challenged them on the need to preach repentance and to "go, and sin no more", have retaliated at her by bizarrely claiming that such biblical truth is deemed to be 'hate speech'. What these so-called shepherds are saying is that preaching repentance is 'preaching hatred'. It is saying that calling people to repent is unloving, unwelcoming and unaccepting. Michele has responded to these people on the lines that, since it is **Jesus Himself** who calls all people to repent of their sins (see Matthew 4:17 & Mark 1:15) and to go and sin no more (see John 8:11), then, drawing a logical conclusion to their thinking, these ministers are basically saying that Jesus Himself hates sinners because it is **He** who calls them to repentance.

Can such ministers not see the folly of their thinking? They claim to be ministers of Christ, but their theology is deeply flawed. Yes we are to love our neighbour as ourselves, but the love of God is not a love that coddles us, patting us on the head and saying that because He loves us so much He will let us do whatever we want, even letting us carry on in our sinful behaviours. But sadly, this is the 'new Christianity', and people love it because they don't want to be made to feel uncomfortable; they just want to feel loved but to be left alone to carry on in their sin. If this is truly what they want then that is exactly what God will let them do whilst they live their life on earth, but they will still have to stand before His throne on the Day of Judgement and give an account to Him of why they refused to believe and obey His Word, preferring instead to live in rebellion to His Word whilst they professed to be a follower of Christ. Let us be clear; this 'new Christianity' is counterfeit Christianity.

Ministers can do whatever they like to try to escape the need to preach about confession and repentance of sin. It will give them an easy job and they will be loved by all for taking this approach, but rebellion is rebellion, no matter how loving it may appear. Rebellion will end in the lake of fire for those who remain unrepentant (see Revelation 21:8).

The few Scripture references that we have included in the paragraphs in this section will give clear evidence that any teaching that **denies** the need for confession and repentance, is a heresy.

Being Born Again

The denial of this foundational truth is escalating in recent times. It was Jesus Himself who said that we must be born again, so when believers think it is not necessary, then they are in serious error (see John Chapter 3). Many are content to have a head-knowledge of what Christianity is about, but they don't want to let go of the reins of their lives and venture into the unknown territory of a born-again relationship with Jesus Christ. Having a head-knowledge of Christ is not going to save our soul from eternity in hell. If Jesus said that we must be born again to enter the kingdom of heaven, then that is one of His conditions. When we travel to a foreign destination, one of the conditions of entry into that country is that we have a passport. If we don't have one, then we will not be allowed into that country, and we will have to remain on the wrong side of the 'arrivals' gate. All our asking and pleading with passport-control staff to let us into our destination will not succeed. This is the perfect description of what Jesus is referring to. In order to enter the kingdom of heaven, one of the biblical conditions is that we must be born again.

Baptism

The subject of baptism seems to be a constant issue in the Church, with many denominations and individual believers having a variety of views and beliefs about it. Many of these views could be held because of our upbringing, or through teaching we have received in certain denominations as well as the tuition we may have received in Theological College. There are many books on the subject of baptism, written by some of the spiritual 'giants' of bygone eras, to which many in the Church may hold their personal beliefs. We take a view that where there is any doubt or confusion regarding baptism, we look for the answers in God's Word. What is the biblical example of baptism and the pattern to which the Church should adhere? Let's have a look at the most important example of all; Jesus' own baptism.

Jesus was baptised in the Jordan River by John the Baptist. John did not feel worthy to undertake this task, but Jesus assured him that he must fulfil it:

"Then Jesus came from Galilee to John at the Jordan [River], to be baptized by him. But John tried to prevent Him [vigorously protesting], saying, "It is I who need to be baptized by You, and do You come to me?" But Jesus replied to him, "Permit it just now; for this is the fitting way for us to fulfill all righteousness." Then John permitted [it and baptized] Him. ***After Jesus was baptized, He came up immediately out of the water;"*** – Matthew 3:13-16(a) AMP (Authors' emphasis)

The fact that Jesus 'came up immediately out of the water' after He was baptised indicates that this would have been a full immersion baptism.

More evidence of this is shown in the following verse:

"And Jesus Christ was revealed as God's Son by ***his baptism in water*** *and by shedding his blood on the cross..."* – 1 John 5:6(a) (Authors' emphasis)

This verse is incredibly important, and one which should not be overlooked in any quarters of the Church, whether that be those in positions of Church leadership, or simply each member of the congregation.

Let's home in on this: The apostle John lists the **importance** of Jesus' baptism **in** water alongside that of the shedding of His blood. This is profound and should make us realise that baptism in water is not just merely an option. There is a deep spiritual significance involved. We read that Jesus is ***'revealed as God's Son by His baptism in water'.*** This raises its importance to a whole new level. Surely then this verse should translate directly to ourselves; that **we** are also revealed as God's sons and daughters by **our** baptism in water.

Also, we see John the Baptist baptising people at a place where there was an abundance of water:

"After these things Jesus and His disciples went into the land of Judea, and there He spent time with them and baptized. Now John was also baptizing at Aenon near Salim, ***because there was an abundance of water there****; and people were coming and were being baptized."* - John 3:22-23 AMP (Authors' emphasis)

We also read that, on the Day of Pentecost, 3,000 people were baptised, and it is highly likely that this was in the same manner as Jesus was baptised:

"So then, those who accepted his message were baptized; and on that day about 3,000 souls were added [to the body of believers]." – Acts 2:41 AMP

Regarding Philip baptising the Ethiopian eunuch, we read:

"As they travelled along the road, they came to some water and the eunuch said, "Look, here is water. What can stand in the way of my being baptized?" And he gave orders to stop the chariot. Then both Philip and the eunuch ***went down into the water and Philip baptized him.*** *"* – Acts 8:36-38 NIV (Authors' emphasis)

The words, *'went down into the water'* would indicate that this was a large body of water.

Saul's baptism is recorded in Acts 9:17-19, and he recounts the experience in Acts 22:16. Whilst it does not mention full immersion baptism, it is almost without doubt that this would have followed the same pattern as that being carried out in other incidents.

The same would most likely apply to the accounts of baptisms being performed in Acts 10:44-48, 16:13-15(a), 18:8, 19:3-5, 22:16.

As followers of Christ, we are to follow Jesus. When He was baptised, He showed us plainly how it was to be fulfilled in our own lives. He has set the example regarding baptism and out of reverence to Him, we should obey His example. Some may consider this to be a legalistic view when many Church denominations have other baptismal options. Having read a little on baptism over the years, it would seem that other methods of baptism may have been introduced over the centuries, most likely to allow for convenience and modesty, according to the societal views and etiquette of those generations. We will admit that neither of us are theologians, but this does not disqualify us from being able to write about this important subject. For us, the place to find the truth on any biblical matter is in the written Word of God. The heart of a faithful believer will endeavour to obey the Word rather than to hold on to any beliefs or teachings that may have been created by the Church for the benefit of modesty and convenience. Some will say that Jesus did not actually say that we are to be baptised by full immersion. No, He may not have spoken those actual words, but **He showed us what to do** by being the example for us to follow. Sometimes, actions speak louder than words.

Having said this, and in order to show that we are not legalistic about this, we will share with you that both of us were baptised as infants, with the sprinkling of water, and we have also been baptised by full immersion as adults. We underwent the latter when we discovered what the Bible had to tell us about being baptised **after** we had become believers (see Mark 16:16). Whilst we had been baptised as infants and were both confirmed into the Church of England in our teenage years, neither of us grew up with any meaningful knowledge of, or relationship with God. It was only when we finally gave our lives to Christ in our adult years and became born again almost 30 years ago, that we finally understood that we needed to fulfil the act of being baptised by full immersion, to mark the burial of our old way of life and being born into our new life in Christ. The realisation of the need to be baptised as a believing adult was a deep conviction given to us by the Holy Spirit, and it brought about in us the need to obey.

We wish to reassure you that we certainly do not trivialise or have negative views of infant baptism. We believe it is important to have children covered with a holy covering as soon as possible after their birth, and therefore believing parents would be doing a spiritually beneficial thing to have their children baptised into the faith of Jesus Christ, or at least dedicated in some way. We believe that something very powerful occurs in the spiritual realm on the occasion of every baptism, whether that be the act of believing parents having their child covered by an infant baptism until the child becomes old enough to understand the Word of God for itself and then makes the decision to be baptised by full immersion at that time, or whether that be the full immersion baptism of a person who comes to faith as an adult.

Whilst, for us, full immersion baptism is shown in the Bible as the biblical way for believers to follow, we do appreciate that the individual circumstances of some people may prevent this from happening, particularly if they are house-bound. Some people may be on their death-bed when they give their lives to Christ and as such it is simply not possible to undertake a full immersion baptism. Allow me to share with you my (Chris) own personal story:

My Father

Whilst my father had been a church-goer for many years, he did not appear outwardly to have a relationship with Jesus. One day, I finally got the chance to have a heart to heart talk with him and, as simply and clearly as I could, I told him the full Gospel story. My father sobbed at the realisation that, for a long time, he had just been going to church but had not understood that he was a sinner in need of salvation. At that moment he gave his life to Christ at the age of 90, a few months before he died. He suffered from advanced stages of Type 2 diabetes and associated conditions as well as dementia. The speed of his decline meant that we were not able to baptise him by full immersion.

With time being of the essence, and feeling compelled by the Lord to swiftly fulfil the duty of baptism, we dispelled with the process of religious formalities and took an empty bottle down to the beach and filled the bottle with some seawater and took it to the hospital. My father was sedated, but knowing that he was most likely able to hear us speaking to him, we told him that because he was now a believer, we were going to baptise him out of obedience to the Lord. So, we conducted a little service in his hospital room, singing some hymns and praying, and then we gently baptised him by washing his arms, legs, head and face with the sea water, in the name of the Father, the Son and the Holy Spirit, as an act of faith of 'washing away his sins' before he died so that he would rise to a new life in Christ. It was a beautiful and deeply meaningful experience. A few days later his soul departed his body to be with the Lord. I have shared this with you to show you that sometimes, out of necessity, circumstances may require us to do something very different in the way of baptism. But for the majority of situations, where we are fully able, it is best to follow the way that Jesus has shown us.

In Acts 22:16, Paul quotes the words that Ananias spoke to him about being baptised:

"Now, why do you delay? Get up and be baptized, and wash away your sins by calling on His name [for salvation]." – Acts 22:16 AMP

Most Christians will understand that baptism is the outward sign that represents the burial of our old way of life, having our sins washed away and rising to a new life in Christ. It is a powerful experience to go through, and, assuming that personal physical limitations do not prohibit it, we encourage all who may still struggle in their beliefs about this issue to simply follow the way of baptism that Jesus showed us. There are times in our journey with the Lord where we may not always understand why we ought to do something. It is at times like this that our obedience to God's Word needs to rise up above our human, natural need to understand.

The Baptism of the Holy Spirit

This is another fiercely debated issue in the Church which many believers have a variety of different views and beliefs about, but again, our source for truth needs to be the Scriptures themselves. We can debate and resist what is written, but it will not negate the fact that God's Word says we need to be 'born of water **and of the Spirit**' (see John 3:5).

In John Chapter 3, Jesus explains that if we choose to follow Him then we need to be changed in a supernatural way. We need to be 'born again'. In effect, He is saying we need to be 're-born' from above. This means that our old life needs to be transformed by God supernaturally. God will not do that unless we ask Him to. The outward sign of this is being baptised with water, which is the 'act'. This is immediately followed by the adoption of a new lifestyle whereby the old self (following the fleshly ways of self, the world and the devil) is 'dead', and the new self (following the ways of God) replaces the old, which is the 'effect'. The act of a believer's baptism is of little value unless it is accompanied by the effect of a change in our lives from that which is of the flesh to that which is in obedience to God's Word. This transformation from the things of the flesh to the things of the Spirit is carried out by the Holy Spirit. As we have pointed out in the verse we referred to above (John 3:5), Jesus says that we must be born of the Spirit for this to happen.

What did He mean?

After Jesus had risen from the dead and appeared to His disciples, but before He had ascended into heaven, He told them that they were not to leave Jerusalem but to await the 'promise of the Father':

"While being together and eating with them, He commanded them not to leave Jerusalem, but to wait for what the Father had promised, "Of which," He said, "you have heard Me speak. For John baptized with water, but you will be baptized and empowered and united with the Holy Spirit, not long from now." – Acts 1:4-5 AMP

In Acts Chapter 2, the Father's promise was indeed poured out upon them in a mighty powerful way. This promise was the infilling of the Holy Spirit, and there was no mistaking that something supernatural had happened to them. One moment they were a frightened bunch of believers huddled in one place for fear of being rounded up by the religious leaders of the time, and the next moment they had all received the baptism of the Holy Spirit which simultaneously enabled them to speak in new tongues (languages which they had never learned). The baptism of the Holy Spirit transformed them from their natural frightened state into men who were suddenly bold, enabling Peter to stand up and preach the Gospel to the crowd, telling them what they must do to be saved. This happened on the Day of Pentecost.

John the Baptist had previously told the people that One would come who would baptise them with the Holy Spirit (see Matthew 3:11 and Luke 3:16). Jesus was this One, and He promised that He would send the Holy Spirit. So after being filled with the Holy Spirit, Peter confirmed to the crowd outside that what they had just seen and heard was the fulfilment of this promise.

When something is promised by someone, our natural instinct is to believe and trust the words of the one who has promised us something. Yet despite Jesus' own promise, many in the Church today do not believe that being filled with the Holy Spirit is even necessary. This is evidenced by the immense lack of teaching on this subject. It is something that ought to be at the forefront of discipleship teaching, yet in most cases it is relegated to an 'optional extra'.

It seems to us that to place no emphasis on this incredible promise of the Father - that is the promise from God Himself – is almost bordering on blasphemy because, in effect, what we are doing is denying the power of the Holy Spirit. If we deny the power of the Holy Spirit, then could it not be deduced that we are denying the existence of the Holy Spirit? It would be a most unusual thing to believe that the Holy Spirit exists but at the same time have absolutely no belief that the Holy Spirit (who is the Spirit of God) has any power to indwell us and transform our lives. We may use the words, 'Holy Spirit' in our services, but if we believe that the baptism of the Holy Spirit is no longer necessary today, and we minimise or even negate the power of the Holy Spirit that is available to all who will believe, then we are merely paying the Holy Spirit lip-service.

Let us look at some Scriptures which show us that being filled with the Holy Spirit was not, and is not just an optional extra:

"When the apostles in Jerusalem heard that [the people of] Samaria had accepted the word of God, they sent Peter and John to them. ***They came down and prayed for them that they might receive the Holy Spirit; for He had not yet fallen on any of them;*** *they had simply been baptized in the name of the Lord Jesus [as His possession]. Then Peter and John laid their hands on them [one by one], and they received the Holy Spirit."* – Acts 8:14-17 AMP (Authors' emphasis)

The words *"for He had not yet fallen on them"* are a direct reference to the Holy Spirit falling on the gathered disciples on the

Day of Pentecost. We surely cannot miss this point! Whilst this passage does not say that they spoke in tongues, we can be almost certain that they did because this was the evidence on the Day of Pentecost after the Holy Spirit **had** fallen on them. God gave them a sign that they had received the baptism of the Holy Spirit. When we personally received the baptism of the Holy Spirit, we began to speak in tongues just like those first believers.

The next passage is from the story of Peter preaching the Gospel to Cornelius and his household. Here we see again the evidence of the baptism of the Holy Spirit:

"While Peter was still speaking these words, ***the Holy Spirit fell on all those who were listening to the message*** *[confirming God's acceptance of Gentiles]. All the circumcised believers who came with Peter were amazed, because the gift of the Holy Spirit had been poured out even on the Gentiles.* ***For they heard them talking in [unknown] tongues (languages) and exalting and magnifying and praising God.****"* – Acts 10:44-46 AMP (Authors' emphasis)

The next passage concerns the believers at Ephesus. They did not know anything about receiving the Holy Spirit, so Paul took the matter in hand:

*"It happened that while Apollos was in Corinth, Paul went through the upper [inland] districts and came down to Ephesus, and found some disciples. He asked them, "****Did you receive the Holy Spirit when you believed [in Jesus as the Christ]****?" And they said, "No, we have not even heard that there is a Holy Spirit." And he asked, "Into what then were you baptized?" They said, "Into John's baptism." Paul said, "John performed a baptism of repentance, continually telling the people to believe in Him who was coming after him, that is, [to confidently accept and joyfully believe] in Jesus [the Messiah and Savior]." After hearing this, they were baptized [again, this time] in the name of the Lord Jesus. And when Paul laid his hands on them,* ***the Holy Spirit came on them, and they began speaking in [unknown] tongues (languages) and prophesying.****"* – Acts 19:1-6 AMP (Authors' emphasis)

This latter passage is clear evidence that many people in the Church are believers and have been baptised in water, but they have not received the baptism of the Holy Spirit. It is so clear how important this is that Paul even asks them if they have received the Holy Spirit **since** they believed! Do our church leaders ask this sort of question of those in their congregations who profess to be believers? Paul was not content to leave them as baptised believers; he wanted them to be filled with the power of the Holy Spirit! Why? Because Paul knew from his own experience (see Acts 8:1-30) that the power of the Holy Spirit living in us transforms, equips and enables us to be God's witnesses in this world, just like the disciples on the Day of Pentecost.

As the baptism of the Holy Spirit is the promise of the Father to His children (those who are followers of His Son Jesus Christ), let us no longer have doubts or unbelief about it, but joyfully accept His promise and receive it for ourselves so that we may bring further glory to His name as He uses us in the power of the Holy Spirit to do more of His works on this earth.

The Spiritual Gifts

Along with the above, there are church leaders who teach that the Spiritual gifts, such as the gift of tongues, interpretation and prophecy, healing, and casting out demons, are 'no longer for today'. Some even say that these gifts are 'of the devil'.

Let's get this straight; the spiritual gifts were given to the Church **by God**, to be used for His glory and were freely used in the early Church, and their reality and practice were written down in Holy Scripture for us all to see. To state that the spiritual gifts are now 'of the devil' must also be bordering on blasphemy against the Holy Spirit, or at the very least this must grieve the Holy Spirit deeply. Can we not see Satan's deception in this?

Such teaching is contrary to the Word of God because Jesus Himself said that 'signs will follow' those **who believe**. They will lay hands on the sick and they will recover, they will cast out demons, and will speak with new tongues (see Mark 16:15-18). When we deny what Jesus has actually stated, we are in a serious state of apostasy and unbelief. Despite this, there are still a great many faithful believers who are filled with the Holy Spirit, who are using these gifts in abundance for the glory of God today!

Taking the Lord's Supper

On the night that He was betrayed, Jesus took the bread and the cup of wine and gave it to His disciples and told them to eat and drink of it in remembrance of Him, until He comes again. (see Matthew 26, Mark 14, Luke 22 and 1 Corinthians 11).

In the passage of 1 Corinthians 11, verse 26 makes mention of taking the bread and wine often; *"for **as often** as you eat this bread and drink this cup..."* (Authors' emphasis). Strangely, some churches feel they have no need to conduct the service of the Lord's Supper (Holy Communion) at all; one church we recently heard about only takes it once a year, and some conduct it in a rather casual and almost irreverent manner. In one church we attended, we witnessed a leader picking up the loaf and smashing it against the table because he was having trouble breaking it in half. This caused people in the congregation to display a somewhat nervous laugh, but quite frankly, we were shocked by this casual, irreverent behaviour. If we think the bread is going to be too difficult to break, let's at least have a knife nearby to cut it with!

Each day, most of us are able to eat food on a daily basis, knowing that what we eat and drink will give us strength for our tasks and will keep our bodies alive and hopefully healthy. When we take Communion – the bread and the wine – we are partaking in the sacred act of eating and drinking the body and blood of Jesus. Jesus is the Bread of Life (see John 6:35), and His blood shed for us is that of the pure, sinless, spotless Lamb of God (see 1 Peter 1:19 NLT). When we eat and drink the communion elements, we are eating and drinking into our beings **His life-giving power**, to cleanse us, forgive us and restore us.

We must take communion in reverence, not with a casual attitude. The apostle Paul had something to say about taking the body and blood of Jesus in an irreverent manner:

"So then whoever eats the bread or drinks the cup of the Lord in a way that is unworthy [of Him] will be guilty of [profaning and sinning against] the body and blood of the Lord. ***But a person must [prayerfully] examine himself [and his relationship to Christ], and only when he has done so should he eat of the bread and drink of the cup. For anyone who eats and drinks [without solemn reverence and heartfelt gratitude for the sacrifice of Christ], eats and drinks a judgment on himself if he does not recognize the body [of Christ].*** *That [careless and unworthy participation] is the reason why many among you are weak and sick, and a number sleep [in death]. But if we evaluated and judged ourselves honestly [recognizing our shortcomings and correcting our behavior], we would not be judged. But when we [fall short and] are judged by the Lord, we are disciplined [by undergoing His correction] so that we will not be condemned [to eternal punishment] along with the world."* – 1 Corinthians 11:27-32 AMP (Authors' emphasis)

It is clear from this passage that taking Communion irreverently - in an unworthy manner - is a matter of the attitude and state of our heart when we come to take the sacraments. Of critical importance is the fact that we need to be a believer in Jesus Christ. We have attended some churches that welcome **all** to the communion table, which may include any unbelievers who are sitting in the pews. The above passage teaches us that we are to examine ourselves first before we even come to the Communion table, to make sure that we have a solemn reverence and heartfelt gratitude for what Jesus did for us on the cross. If we go to church but do not feel this way about Jesus, or in our heart we know that we are not really a believer, then we should **not** take Communion, even if the minister says that we can. The minister will be in error for encouraging participation in taking Communion in a light-hearted manner, and the consequences of taking it without reverence are serious.

The Reality of Hell

Despite Jesus teaching a huge amount on the reality of hell in the four Gospels and the Book of Revelation, and also the apostles doing likewise in the rest of the New Testament, it seems beyond belief that anyone in the Church could deny the reality of hell, or dismiss this biblical fact as a mere 'fantasy' or a 'scare story'. Yet many Christians do think this, preferring to only believe in heaven. Below are some Scriptures for you to look up in your own Bible, which tell us clearly that hell is real. They are Jesus' own Words, and they apply not just to unbelievers but also to anyone who claims to be a follower of Christ, but whose lifestyle displays that they are more a follower of Satan.

See the following:

Matthew 10:28, 13:42, 22:13, 25:30; Mark 9:44-48; Luke 13:28; 2 Peter 2:4; Revelation 20:15 & 22:14-16

So, after reading these, if you think that you might be on the highway to hell, we urge you to repent, **now**, for the sake of your eternal destiny. You are playing 'Russian Roulette' with the salvation of your soul. God does not want any to perish, but for all to come to repentance so that they can be saved (see 2 Peter 3:9). But it is up to us to make this choice. God will not force us to. We are the ones who must choose between heaven and hell. God has provided for us the free gift of eternal life through His Son Jesus Christ, but it is up to us to accept His gift, and to live our lives with faith in Jesus. If we reject His gift, then Scripture is clear, eternity in hell will be our destination.

The Reality of Jesus' Second Coming

It is simply staggering to discover that many in the Church do not really believe in the Second Coming of Christ, or that those who once believed this truth have since abandoned all thought of it for a variety of reasons.

Peter points out such people,

"Most importantly, I want to remind you that in the last days scoffers will come, mocking the truth and following their own desires. They will say, "What happened to the promise that Jesus is coming again? From before the times of our ancestors, everything has remained the same since the world was first created." – 2 Peter 3:3-4

No amount of showing people the Scriptures seems to have any effect on convincing them of the error of their unbelief. The disciples actually asked Jesus what the signs would be of His coming, and He told them plainly in the whole of Matthew Chapter 24, yet still many in the Church do not believe He will return. Below are some further Scriptures from the New Testament confirming the truth that He is going to return.

At Jesus' ascension into heaven,

"They were looking intently up into the sky as he was going, when suddenly two men dressed in white stood beside them. "Men of Galilee," they said, "why do you stand here looking into the sky? This same Jesus, who has been taken from you into heaven, will come back in the same way you have seen him go into heaven." – Acts 1:10-11 NIV

Concerning Jesus' return, Paul says,

"Now concerning how and when all this will happen, dear brothers and sisters, we don't really need to write you. For you know quite well that the day of the Lord's return will come unexpectedly, like a thief in the night. When people are saying, "Everything is peaceful and secure," then disaster will fall on them as suddenly as a pregnant woman's labor pains begin. And there will be no escape." – 1 Thessalonians 5:1-3

In the Book of Revelation, the angel of the Lord said to the apostle John,

"BEHOLD, HE IS COMING WITH THE CLOUDS, and every eye will see Him, even those who pierced Him; and all the tribes (nations) of the earth will mourn over Him [realizing their sin and guilt, and

anticipating the coming wrath]. So it is to be. Amen." – Revelation 1:7 AMP

Jesus is going to return whether we believe it or not, and whether we are ready or not. We cannot say that the Scriptures have not warned us of this.

So, having looked at all these foundational truths, which many in the Church are denying, if we are among those who deny all or any of them, we are utterly deceived, and desperately need to wake ourselves up, shake ourselves up and seek the Lord with all our mind, heart and soul, asking Him to reach down and rescue us from our shocking state of apostasy.

To sum up this shocking state, Hill gives us some information, collated in 1963 at the conference of the National Council of Churches of Christ, regarding the basic beliefs of clergy and laity who attended. He says,

'Sociologist Jeffrey Hadden did a survey of ministers of a mainline denomination in the USA that showed some startling levels of unbelief among church leaders…

The results of his survey are reproduced below.' [9]

Basic Beliefs of Clergy and Laity

	ORDAINED MINISTERS		LAITY
	In Administrative Positions	In Pastoral Charge	
BELIEF IN: (No doubts)	%	%	%
God	60	62	78
Divinity of Christ	54	60	71
Life After Death	58	70	70
Virgin Birth	22	27	46
The Devil	18	28	7
Original Sin	11	22	17
Miracles	16	24	33

If this was the spiritual condition of ministers in the Church on these foundational issues in the 1960's, with what we are now seeing in the Church today, one can only imagine the depths of unbelief to which it has further fallen.

As of the time of writing (July 2019), at the General Synod of the Anglican Church of Canada, 80.9% of the Order of Laity, 73.2% of the Order of Clergy and 62.2% of the Order of Bishops voted **in favour** of same-sex marriage, although this needed a two-thirds majority in all three Orders for it to be passed. So, for now, only by a whisker, the Anglican Church of Canada still retains traditional marriage between a man and a woman. But with the way things are heading throughout the worldwide Church, we are sure that the next time the General Synod convenes, the sacred covenant of Holy Matrimony being solely between a biological man and a biological woman will be overturned by those attending the meeting, and marriage in the Church will be made available for all types of relationships in the name of inclusion, equality and progress.

For further information on this issue, see:

http://anglican.ink/2019/07/13/gay-marriage-rejected-by-canadian-synod-bishops-reject-resolution-by-one-vote/

Chapter 4 - Section C

Replacement Theology & Antisemitism in the Church; The 'gospel' of Universalism; Worldly-style worship; Strange Activities in the Church

Replacement Theology & Antisemitism in the Church

It is not the intention of this book to enter into any deep discussion on the subject of this heading, but because antisemitism is an issue that is constantly in the news headlines, causing many in the Church to distance themselves from having any views concerning Israel, we feel it best for you to read some of the passages from God's Word concerning His beloved nation Israel.

Let us begin by explaining what is meant by Replacement Theology. Essentially, Replacement Theology teaches that the Church is the replacement for Israel and that the many promises made to Israel in the Bible are now fulfilled in the Christian Church, and not Israel because of its rejection of the Messiah, Jesus Christ. Replacement Theology suggests that Jews are no longer God's chosen people and that God does not have specific future plans for the nation of Israel. (see www.gotquestions.org)

Whilst this subject is an issue that has been a part of the Christian Church for a very long time, over the past few decades, the Church seems to have failed to teach believers about the history of the Jews, and how it came about that salvation was made available to the Gentile nations. We say this from our own experience, having spent three-quarters of our lives to date as followers of Christ but with absolutely no interest in Church history, until 2011, when God started to reveal things to us, which caused the veil to drop from our eyes regarding Israel.

With many in today's Church not having much interest in or knowledge concerning the Jewish roots of Christianity, over the past few years particularly there seems to have been a resurgence of antisemitic thinking within the 'progressive' Church of our times.

As followers of Christ, let us first remind ourselves that, in the Bible, God is known as the 'God of Israel' (see Exodus 5:1, Matthew 15:31, & Luke 1:68). Let us also remind ourselves that God's Son, Jesus Christ (known as Yeshua HaMashiach to Jews who have received Him as their Saviour), was a Jew and raised in a Jewish household, observing all of the Jewish customs (see Luke Chapter 2), and teaching in the synagogues. We also know from Scripture that His first disciples were all Jewish, as He referred to them as 'brothers' (for example, see Matthew Chapter 4). It would not have been the custom in those times to refer to people of gentile nations as 'brothers'. Some believe that Luke (who wrote the Gospel of Luke and the Book of Acts) was a Gentile believer, but all the other New Testament writers were Jewish believers.

With this basic knowledge, and with the Scripture passages below, we will clearly see that Replacement Theology is a false gospel; a heresy. It is one of Satan's most evil deceptions, which is raising its ugly head in the Christian Church, deceiving many into believing that God has abandoned and forsaken the Children of Israel because of their rejection of His Son, Jesus Christ, Yeshua HaMashiach.

Let's make this clear: God has **not** 'replaced' Israel with the Gentile followers of Christ in the Christian Church! In God's mercy for the Gentile believers, He has 'grafted us in' to His plan of salvation. To 'graft something in', means that the original 'stock' is still there, as the main root. The 'grafted in' part is just a branch attached to the main rootstock. God has not dug up His beloved Israel and discarded her onto the trash heap. His love and mercy for her remains the same as it did at the beginning, and He will not forsake her.

For the Christian Church to believe the antisemitic doctrine of Replacement Theology, and to begin expressing it in agreeing with the application of BDS (Boycott, Divestment and Sanctions) against Israel, is to actually enter into what most of the world is now doing to Israel on an escalating basis. The world, and much of the Church, is **cursing** Israel, and God has got something to say about it, as we will now see.

Speaking to Abraham, God said,

"I will make you into a great nation. I will bless you and make you famous, and you will be a blessing to others. I will bless those who bless you and curse those who treat you with contempt. All the families on earth will be blessed through you." – Genesis 12:2-3

God is saying that He will curse those who curse Israel. This is not just a warning to the nations of the world who currently curse Israel with BDS, with some nations even expressing a desire to wipe Israel off the map; it is also a warning to followers of Christ in the Christian Church who get involved in any practice that directly or indirectly curses or harms Israel. We must fall on our faces in repentance immediately, or face the consequences, as individuals, corporately as the Church, and also as nations. God is watching us.

Let's look at what Paul wrote to the believers in Rome concerning the matter of God's chosen people, Israel. We will see that, right from the start, the early Church was being deceived with this insidious doctrine of Replacement Theology. But what excuse does the Church today have in keeping this lie alive when we have God-inspired Holy Scripture, which we are about to read, to rebuke us and correct our thinking?

It is a long passage, but we exhort you to read all of it, because only then will we be able to escape from Satan's lie about Israel, when we come to the knowledge of the truth from God's Word.

God's Mercy on Israel

"I ask, then, has God rejected his own people, the nation of Israel? Of course not! I myself am an Israelite, a descendant of Abraham and a member of the tribe of Benjamin.

No, God has not rejected his own people, whom he chose from the very beginning. Do you realize what the Scriptures say about this? Elijah the prophet complained to God about the people of Israel and said, "LORD, they have killed your prophets and torn down your altars. I am the only one left, and now they are trying to kill me, too."

And do you remember God's reply? He said, "No, I have 7,000 others who have never bowed down to Baal!"

It is the same today, for a few of the people of Israel have remained faithful because of God's grace — his undeserved kindness in choosing them. And since it is through God's kindness, then it is not by their good works. For in that case, God's grace would not be what it really is — free and undeserved.

So this is the situation: Most of the people of Israel have not found the favor of God they are looking for so earnestly. A few have — the ones God has chosen — but the hearts of the rest were hardened. As the Scriptures say,

"God has put them into a deep sleep.

To this day he has shut their eyes so they do not see, and closed their ears so they do not hear."

Likewise, David said,

"Let their bountiful table become a snare,
a trap that makes them think all is well.
Let their blessings cause them to stumble,
and let them get what they deserve.

Let their eyes go blind so they cannot see, and let their backs be bent forever."

Did God's people stumble and fall beyond recovery? Of course not! They were disobedient, so God made salvation available to the Gentiles. But he wanted his own people to become jealous and claim it for themselves. Now if the Gentiles were enriched because the people of Israel turned down God's offer of salvation, think how much greater a blessing the world will share when they finally accept it.

I am saying all this especially for you Gentiles. God has appointed me as the apostle to the Gentiles. I stress this, for I want somehow to make the people of Israel jealous of what you Gentiles have, so I might save some of them. For since their rejection meant that God offered salvation to the rest of the world, their acceptance will be even more wonderful. It will be life for those who were dead! And since Abraham and the other patriarchs were holy, their descendants will also be holy — just as the entire batch of dough is holy because the portion given as an offering is holy. For if the roots of the tree are holy, the branches will be, too.

But some of these branches from Abraham's tree — some of the people of Israel — have been broken off. And you Gentiles, who were branches from a wild olive tree, have been grafted in. So now you also receive the blessing God has promised Abraham and his children, sharing in the rich nourishment from the root of God's special olive tree. But you must not brag about being grafted in to replace the branches that were broken off. You are just a branch, not the root.

"Well," you may say, "those branches were broken off to make room for me." Yes, but remember — those branches were broken off because they didn't believe in Christ, and you are there because you do believe. So don't think highly of yourself, but fear what could happen. For if God did not spare the original branches, he won't spare you either.

Notice how God is both kind and severe. He is severe toward those who disobeyed, but kind to you if you continue to trust in his kindness. But if you stop trusting, you also will be cut off. And if the people of Israel turn from their unbelief, they will be grafted in again, for God has the power to graft them back into the tree. You, by nature, were a branch cut from a wild olive tree. So if God was willing to do something contrary to nature by grafting you into his cultivated tree, he will be far more eager to graft the original branches back into the tree where they belong.

I want you to understand this mystery, dear brothers and sisters, so that you will not feel proud about yourselves. Some of the people of Israel have hard hearts, but this will last only until the full number of Gentiles comes to Christ. And so all Israel will be saved. As the Scriptures say,

"The one who rescues will come from Jerusalem,
and he will turn Israel away from ungodliness.
And this is my covenant with them,
that I will take away their sins."

Many of the people of Israel are now enemies of the Good News, and this benefits you Gentiles. Yet they are still the people he loves because he chose their ancestors Abraham, Isaac, and Jacob. For God's gifts and his call can never be withdrawn." – Romans 11:1-29

This is the Word of the Lord, and we will leave it do its convicting work in the hearts of those in the Church whose eyes have been veiled to this truth.

The 'gospel' of Universalism

"I am astonished and extremely irritated that you are so quickly shifting your allegiance and deserting Him who called you by the grace of Christ, for a different [even contrary] gospel; which is really not another [gospel]; but there are [obviously] some [people masquerading as teachers] who are disturbing and confusing you [with a misleading, counterfeit teaching] and want to distort the gospel of Christ [twisting it into something which it absolutely is not]. But even if we, or an angel from heaven, should preach to you a gospel contrary to that which we [originally] preached to you, let him be condemned to destruction! As we have said before, so I now say again, if anyone is preaching to you a gospel different from that which you received [from us], let him be condemned to destruction! Am I now trying to win the favor and approval of men, or of God? Or am I seeking to please someone? If I were still trying to be popular with men, I would not be a bond-servant of Christ." – Galatians 1:6-10 AMP

Rather interestingly, the Google definition of Universalism is: "**Christian Theology** - the belief that all humankind will eventually be saved." (Authors' emphasis). Let's make one thing very clear; Universalism has nothing to do with Christian Theology whatsoever, as we will now show you.

Doing a general online search will show that the deception of Universalism teaches that all humanity will be saved and restored to a right relationship with God, regardless of whether we sin or not, and whatever we believe or don't believe. We would like to make another thing clear; that statement is a lie of Satan which every believer can discover for themselves if they will simply read the written Word of God. In His Word, we will find that there is no automatic entry into heaven when we die; there is no automatic salvation for every soul. Salvation and eternal life are the promised inheritance of all who believe in and have faith in the One who died on the cross to set them free from sin and eternal punishment in hell (see John 3:16). The One who did this, for the whole human race throughout the whole world, is Jesus Christ, who is the Messiah (see Matthew 16:16).

The complete work of salvation is finished; it happened at Calvary, on the cross, where Jesus was crucified (see John Chapter 19). From that point on, salvation was and has been made **available** for all, no matter who we are or where we come from; but again, we must stress that inheriting eternal life is **not** our 'automatic right'. In order to receive this free gift of salvation and eternal life, we must believe in, have faith in, and follow and obey Jesus Christ, the One who gave His life for us.

In the Amplified Bible, the apostle John says,

"For God so [greatly] loved and dearly prized the world, that He [even] gave His [One and] only begotten Son, so that whoever believes and trusts in Him [as Savior] shall not perish, but have eternal life. For God did not send the Son into the world to judge and condemn the world [that is, to initiate the final judgment of the world], but that

the world might be saved through Him. Whoever believes and has decided to trust in Him [as personal Savior and Lord] is not judged [for this one, there is no judgment, no rejection, no condemnation]; but the one who does not believe [and has decided to reject Him as personal Savior and Lord] is judged already [that one has been convicted and sentenced], because he has not believed and trusted in the name of the [One and] only begotten Son of God [the One who is truly unique, the only One of His kind, the One who alone can save him]. This is the judgment [that is, the cause for indictment, the test by which people are judged, the basis for the sentence]: the Light has come into the world, and people loved the darkness rather than the Light, for their deeds were evil. For every wrongdoer hates the Light, and does not come to the Light [but shrinks from it] for fear that his [sinful, worthless] activities will be exposed and condemned." – John 3:16-20 AMP

Salvation is through no other (see Acts 4:11-12). As the above Scripture clearly shows, if we do not believe or we refuse to accept God's gift to us through faith in Jesus, we are condemned to judgement, and we will get the shock of our life when our soul leaves our body at the point of death.

Satan wants us to believe that because God created the whole human race, God will let the souls of the whole human race into heaven when we die. This lie sounds quite convincing, doesn't it? But this is not the truth according to God's Word. Yes, all people are created in God's image (see Genesis 1:27), and God created the first human beings as perfect, but after Adam and Eve fell for Satan's deception in the Garden of Eden, as we have said before, the whole human race from that day onwards has been born with the inherent disposition of sin, and eternity in hell is the default position of all that is sinful and evil (see Revelation 21:27).

We personally cannot change this through our own efforts. We cannot get rid of this disposition ourselves; we need someone to save us from our sins. Matthew 1:18-25 shows us that the angel of the Lord declared to Joseph that Jesus would save His people (the Jews) from their sins. In Acts Chapter 10, this salvation was then made available to all who become believers from the Gentile nations.

Because of our inherent sin resulting from The Fall of Adam and Eve, God has also banished us from His presence and from 'paradise'. The only way back for the whole human race is through the 'Door of Salvation' that God has opened, which is through faith in His Son, Jesus Christ (see John 10:1-17). In our stubbornness and pride, we try to gain entry through a multitude of other 'doors' that do not involve having faith in Jesus, but none of these 'doors' will give us entry into God's heavenly kingdom.

If 'all will be saved' regardless of our religious beliefs or none, then based on this line of thinking, God sent His Son Jesus to us and He was crucified and shed His blood for **nothing**. This shows that the 'gospel' of Universalism is a lie from the pit of hell, as this kind of 'salvation' negates the cross of Christ. The Scriptures are clear; Jesus' death on the cross opened the door of salvation and eternal life for all humanity but it is only given to those who admit that they are sinners in need of His saving mercy and grace, who then turn to Him, trust in Him and follow Him. If someone holds a gift in their hands and offers it to us but we reject it and do not take it out of their hands, then we will not benefit from the gift that they are wanting to give us. The gift is still there and is still available to us if we will accept it, but our unwillingness to receive it prevents us from enjoying its benefits. Universalism rejects Jesus' gift of salvation through faith in Him and instead promotes that all will be saved no matter what.

Universalism's teaching is designed to soothe us with the lie that we don't need to repent of our sins, and that God is not a God of wrath, judgement or justice. People are getting sucked into this heretical teaching, including many followers of Christ, who want an 'easy walk' rather than the discipline of obedience to God's Word.

Universalism is deceiving millions of people who do not want to be convicted by the Holy Word of God that we are all sinners in God's sight, and in need of salvation through faith in the only Saviour whom God sent to us. His name is Jesus Christ. He is the Messiah. There is no other name by which we can be saved from eternity in hell.

"For Jesus is the one referred to in the Scriptures, where it says, 'The stone that you builders rejected has now become the cornerstone.' There is salvation in no one else! God has given no other name under heaven by which we must be saved." – Acts 4:11-12

The heresy of Universalism has been around for centuries, but it would seem that lately it has risen to new heights with the proliferation of books and movies that peddle this deception. We are stunned when we read articles that highlight the glaringly obvious apostasy of a growing number of Christian leaders who endorse such material, thereby causing their congregations to buy these books, or to rush to the latest 'blockbuster' movie version of such books.

Universalism is a snake from the pit of hell, which will entice you into its lair. Followers of Christ need to immerse themselves in the Word of God in order to discern the deception that is in front of their eyes when they read and watch these things, promoted under the label of 'Christianity'. Many are drawn to the 'feel good' factor that these books and movies have in bucket loads. We all like a good story, but as Christians, it is vital that the message we believe is the truth of God's Word, **not** these counterfeits.

Universalism's teaching is that we are all on a path to heaven; a path that is big enough and wide enough for everyone to fit on, and no one will be excluded. This sounds very much like the 'mutual flourishing' that we mentioned in Section B.

Here are the Words of Jesus on this very matter:

*"Enter through the narrow gate. **For wide is the gate and broad***

and easy to travel is the path that leads the way to destruction and eternal loss, and there are many who enter through it. *But small is the gate and narrow and difficult to travel is the path that leads the way to [everlasting] life, and there are few who find it."* Matthew 7:13-14 AMP (Authors' emphasis)

It is clear from Jesus' Word where the wide path of Universalism will end.

Worldly-style worship

It seems that many churches today feel that the only way they will ever get people into the church is to offer them a style of worship that is more like a worldly 'gig' than a time of reverential worship to our Holy God. Today's modern 'pop band' style of worship is designed to attract today's unbelievers and younger people. Some of this may be reverential, but there is also a lot going on which is making it hard to distinguish church worship bands from the bands of the secular world. Ramped up music, flashing light systems, and smoke machines billowing out, engulfing the band and the audience, supposedly to create an ethereal, heavenly 'atmosphere'.

Why is the traditional worship, that brought in millions of people to have an encounter with Christ in bygone eras, now viewed as antiquated and even boring by some Christians in the 21st century Church? The reverential worship of the powerful lyrics of many of the old hymns brought people to their knees under the power of the Holy Spirit, bringing upon them a conviction that they were sinners who needed to confess and repent of their sins and turn to Christ to save them.

We need worship that truly honours God. We have heard people say things like, "Oh, I didn't think much of the worship tonight. It didn't do much for me." Brothers and sisters, we are not supposed to be at a worship service for what **we** can get out of it. We are there to worship **God** and give glory to Him. The feelings that we should experience in a worship service - where we are in the presence of our

Holy God - are a sense of our unworthiness to be standing before Him other than through the blood of His son Jesus Christ, and the overwhelming conviction of any ongoing unrepentant sin which will lead to confession and repentance. After having experienced these things, we are then able to feel the joy of God's mercy, grace and forgiveness, and give Him our thanks and praise.

When we look at social media and watch some of the things that are being promoted as Christian worship, we are often lost for words, as we see some worship leaders unsuitably dressed to attract fans who have come to the event to see **them** perform rather than to worship God. Our Christian forefathers must be watching from the ramparts of heaven in shock and grief that believers could forget why they have come to worship, and instead place their eyes on the idol of their affection rather than on God Himself.

Let's get back to the reason why we are worshipping. It is to come into the presence of God, broken as we are, and to give Him praise, glory and thanks that we are able to do so through the blood of Jesus Christ. We are not there for our own pleasure, and we are certainly not there for any kind of 'entertainment'. When our focus is on what we can get out of it, we are coming with the wrong motive.

And as for our attitude to the kind of worship music that we think God is pleased with, throwing out the old for the sake of the new is purely a matter of our personal taste. How can we possibly be the decider on what type of worship music and songs God delights in?! If we are to come to God as little children, then He would be pleased with the most basic of worship. If our only instrument was to bang a wooden spoon on a plastic tub whilst singing "Jesus loves me, this I know", then we feel certain that all of heaven would join in singing with us, creating a mighty orchestra and choir in the heavens that would thunder its way into God's throne room!

It may sound like we are saying this in jest, but we are not. As Christians, we need to see with our spiritual eyes that if every prayer that we pray is lifted up to the throne room of God (see Psalm 141:1-2 and Revelation 8:4), then every song that we sing in worship – whether it is the full repertoire of 'Handel's Messiah' or the simple chorus of 'Jesus loves me, this I know' - must also surely rise up into the heavenly realms too, and make its way into the presence of God who is surrounded by His holy angels, who are worshipping Him night and day. Many of the Psalms are overflowing with worship to God, and He longs to hear our sincere and heartfelt worship, however gifted or imperfect it may be. God is looking at our **heart** as we worship, not whether we have a perfectly polished ability to perform. God receives and delights in all of our worship, no matter how 'rusty' it may sound to our own ears, which are often only content with hearing something that sounds like perfection. Just because we may not like some kinds of simple worship songs, or ones that we consider dated, it does not mean that God feels the same about them. Let us come before Him and worship Him, with both hymns of old and songs that are new; with rousing 'roof-raisers' and simple choruses; but let us do so with reverence and fear of His holiness.

"Because of your unfailing love, I can enter your house; I will worship at your Temple with deepest awe." – Psalm 5:7

"O come, let us worship and bow down, Let us kneel before the Lord our Maker [in reverent praise and prayer]." – Psalm 95:6 AMP

"Shout with joy before the Lord, O earth! Obey him gladly; come before him, singing with joy. Try to realize what this means—the Lord is God! He made us—we are his people, the sheep of his pasture. Go through his open gates with great thanksgiving; enter his courts with praise. Give thanks to him and bless his name." – Psalm 100:1-4 TLB

"Let us go to the sanctuary of the LORD; let us worship at the footstool of his throne." – Psalm 132:7

"...let us show gratitude, and offer to God pleasing service and acceptable worship with reverence and awe; for our God is [indeed] a consuming fire." – Hebrews 12:28(b)-29 AMP

Strange Activities in Church - to Embrace the Community

As the days, weeks and months go by we are seeing more and more strange things occurring in churches, which quite frankly, leave us stunned and shaking our heads in disbelief. On social media, we have come across articles showing some churches setting up a bar and selling alcohol in the church to attract people in. We also read an article that a church was having cannabis services, claiming that using it enhances their times of worship. It would seem to us that creating ways to do these things in a church service is more rooted in wanting people to be free to come into the church without having to give up their ungodly lifestyles.

The Church does need to find ways of encouraging unbelievers to come in, with all their worldly passions and desires, but we should do so without turning our church services into an 'affirming' social event. We must also find a way of introducing newcomers to the biblical teaching of confession and repentance of sin. When we fail to do this, what we are actually doing is giving sin unhindered access into the House of God. Unchecked and unrepentant sin in the Church will eventually bring about its downfall.

Evangelism 'Tools'

Recently, a mega-church promoted a 'helicopter Easter egg drop' to bring in the crowds, and another turned their worship centre into a full-scale boxing ring. We read of one church that bought a whole fleet of brand-new cars and told people to come in and take them away!

Our eyes always pop out of our heads when we read what churches are doing under the label of 'evangelism'. These over-the-top worldly attractions labelled 'evangelism tools' are used to get people through the door in their thousands. Of course people will come to our churches if they think they are in with a chance of driving away in a brand new car! But take those gimmicks away, and the next week those thousands of people may not be anywhere in sight. Huge sums of money is being spent on these attractions when that money could be used more effectively to bring the Gospel to the poor and the destitute, including offering a hot meal and a drink to those who have nothing, and perhaps even housing some of them.

We do not wish to knock the generosity of these mega-churches, but surely we need to get back to the simple preaching of the Gospel and trusting in God that the Power of the Holy Spirit will do His work to bring conviction of sin, confession and repentance upon those who walk through the church doors, whether that be thousands of people, or just one. We believe that the Church should stop using the methods of the world to attract people in. They may flock in to partake of our gimmicks, but if they don't like the Gospel message that we then preach to them, they will vanish as quickly as the morning mist.

Cathedrals

In the United Kingdom, we have read in the media of a Cathedral turning the place of worship into a cinema, showing films that can only be described as pagan and pornographic. Their reason for doing this? – It was claimed by the Dean that the Cathedral is a place for everybody and it needs to serve as wide a range of people as possible; needing to be open to new people; that it doesn't belong just to those who go to church or religious people; that it doesn't belong to those in positions of authority in the Cathedral. This shockingly defensive response caused an uproar, and quite rightly. The Cathedral is the House of God in a community. It belongs to **Him**, not the community. All who come into it should respect what the Cathedral is and come in to worship God, or at least quietly walk around to view the architecture. It should **not** be turned into a glorified community hall for all manner of unsavoury, godless activities just to please people and get them through the door! Having screened these pornographic films, Holy Communion was then to take place the next morning, in seats where people were sitting the previous night, watching films that no doubt would have aroused all manner of erotic feelings. How can any person in high office in the Church justify the showing of gratuitous sex scenes, followed by Holy Communion a few hours later?! Have our Church leaders lost their minds?! Are these leaders really born again and baptised in the Holy Spirit? It would seem not. "By their fruit you will know them." (see Matthew 7:16-20)

Another Cathedral decided to allow the Islamic call to prayer and the reading of the Koran to take place in a Christian service, in the name of 'multi-faith inclusivity'. After huge outrage by the church community, the staff of that Cathedral has since stated that it won't repeat this practice.

Yet another Cathedral turned its sanctuary into a mini-golf course for the summer season, and as of the time of typing this, news has broken of a Cathedral erecting a fifty-foot tall helter-skelter inside the building! And then we hear of a gin and prosecco festival being held in the grounds of a Cathedral.

In John Bunyan's classic work *'The Pilgrim's Progress'* he tells the story of being led off the path to the Celestial City and into a place of amusements, called 'Vanity Fair'. We have no hesitation in saying that we believe that all these worldly things coming into the Church today is 'Vanity Fair' being set up right in the very sanctuary of the House of God. Christians no longer have to leave the Church to wander off the straight and narrow path; they can now be led off the path right in the very heart of the Church itself.

This is all being done under the banner of welcoming people, in the 'hope' that they might say a prayer or light a candle, or maybe think of God. Many people will go into a Cathedral or church building to do something if it is encouraging them in with the offer of worldly attractions, but to hope that this in itself might somehow bring them to a knowledge of God and their need for salvation, is a stretch too far. Nothing but the preaching of the Gospel and the power of the Holy Spirit will achieve this, so a fairground ride and a glass of bubbly is not going to do the trick!

We wrote a little poem about this:

> "The Watchmen are sounding the warnings, but the shepherds have morphed into wolves.
>
> No longer teaching the dangers of sin, repentance, or saving of souls.
>
> Preferring to offer mini-golf and helter-skelters to appeal to the sheep;
>
> Judgement is coming; when Jesus returns, will He find us AWAKE…
>
> or asleep?"

Covering up the Cross

We read about a church which planned to host a Muslim dinner event and said that it would cover up all crosses and any Christian items in the church so as not to 'cause offense'. This church also offered two segregated places **within** the church building where Muslim men and women could pray to Allah separately. It is one thing to host a meal for those of other religions, but it is quite another when we offer to hide the cross and other Christian items so as not to offend them, and allow prayer to foreign gods in the place where we worship Jesus Christ as the Messiah and our Lord and Saviour, whom those of the Muslim religion believe only to be a prophet.

Jesus has a strong warning for those who are ashamed of Him:

"For whoever is ashamed [here and now] of Me and My words, the Son of Man will be ashamed of him when He comes in His glory and the glory of the [heavenly] Father and of the holy angels." – Luke 9:26 AMP

Also on this same matter, The Right Reverend Dr Gavin Ashenden, says,

'Covering the cross or any Christian symbol to placate those who reject Him is in fact a most serious betrayal. Christians who out of a misplaced generosity are more faithful to the Mohammed's requirements than to Jesus' claims risk being separated from God forever. They will have to choose between Mohammed and Jesus.' [10]

Interestingly, this same scenario occurred in the Church of Sweden in 2015 where the world's first openly lesbian female bishop called for a church to remove all signs of the cross and instead build an Islamic prayer room in the chapel, to make it more 'comfortable' for Muslim immigrants who arrive.

And just recently, we have read of a minister in a main denominational Church in Canada, who is outspokenly an atheist and declared this fact from the pulpit. This minister does not recognise the Bible as being more authoritative than other sources and states that they rarely read the Bible in services. The obvious question arises; how did this person ever get selected, let alone ordained to be a minister in a Christian Church?

New Age Classes

We have read of churches advertising New Age classes such as eastern meditation and mindfulness based on Buddhism, as well as hypnotherapy, hypnosis, and spiritualist healings of various sorts. This type of thing should **not be happening in any church**. Where is our discernment?! The church noticeboard should not be used to promote anything that is not in keeping with God's Word, let alone allow the church building to be used for these purposes. Church leaders should be signposting non-Christian organisations to put their adverts on community hall noticeboards instead.

Many churches are encouraging Yoga to take place on their premises, now being promoted as 'Christian Yoga'. The origins of Yoga are rooted in the eastern religious practices of Hinduism where the yoga movements are postures that are offered to the millions of Hindu gods. Christians should not be involved in this. For more information on this, check out an article by Laura Bagby, on the website www1.cbn.com/health/should-christians-do-yoga

Tarot cards and Mediums

We have recently read of some churches using 'Christian tarot cards' as a means for 'guiding' people's lives. Is the Bible no longer good enough?! A church in America has appointed a psychic medium on to its ministerial staff. This person claims to be able to commune with the dead, as a way to bring comfort for those in the church who have lost loved ones. She claims that God 'told her' to do this, yet God's Word actually says the exact opposite! The Scriptures tell us quite clearly that necromancy – consulting with mediums to contact the spirits of the dead - is something that no one who calls themselves a follower of Christ should ever do. Here are a few Scriptures to check out:

Leviticus 19:26(b) & 31, Leviticus 20:6, Deuteronomy 18:10-14, 1 Chronicles 10:11-14, Isaiah 8:19-20, Luke 16:24-26, 1 Timothy 2:4-6

Witchcraft

We have recently read articles on social media about 'Christian witches'; people who say that it is perfectly compatible to be both a Christian and a witch, yet with the same breath they say that the Bible is a 'book of sorcery'! They even hold 'Christian witches' conferences, and have their own personal website. Once upon a time, spiritual watchmen would have ensured that such demonic statements and practices were stamped out. The problem is that many of our watchmen have turned into wolves and are happy to permit such heresy to dwell in the House of God, in the name of allowing people to use their 'spiritual' gifts! God's spiritual gifts are listed in the Bible – witchcraft **is not** one of them!

Drag queen Story Hour and Pride Parades

And finally, as we write this, we have come across a church that has taken to hosting a 'drag queen' story hour, teaching children about the LGBTQ+ agenda. This leads on to the increasing number of churches who are now marching with and celebrating the LGBTQ+ Pride parades; an event that was originally just for one day, then a weekend, then a week, but now occupying a whole month.

Yes, we are called to love all, and to reach out to them with the Gospel message of salvation through faith in Jesus Christ in the hope that some will come to their senses and recognize that their lifestyle is sinful, repent of their sin and be saved. But followers of Christ are **not** called to immerse themselves in joyfully embracing, celebrating, and condoning the sin that is being unashamedly and proudly flaunted during these parades. We have briefly seen video clips of people expressing overly sexualised movements whilst on these parades, which no follower of Christ should be a part of. Yes, we must go where sin is being promoted and practiced in order to plead with those in sin to flee from the fires of hell, but we must not stay there and join in their party.

Nudity

And just when you thought you had heard it all, we have recently read an article about a church in America that is encouraging its flock to come to church and 'bare all'. Using the basis of 'equality', the pastor has succeeded in getting his congregants to strip off and embrace the freedom of nude worship. Using the flimsiest of 'reasons' to validate this practice, the church says that God is okay with nude worship because Jesus was born naked, died naked and rose from the dead naked. It would seem they have forgotten that, after The Fall in the Garden of Eden, when Adam and Eve realised that they were naked, God Himself made garments for them to cover their nakedness. For more information on this article, search on the Internet for 'White Tail Chapel, Southampton, Virginia'.

This concludes our look at some of the strange activities that are occurring in the Church in our times, although by the time this book is released for sale, we are sure many more strange things will be happening.

Much of the Church is now on a rapid trajectory of preferring to embrace the whole gamut of concepts and ideologies of political correctness and mutual flourishing, under the guise of freedom for all. However, in all of these circumstances, God expects all in the Church to use and apply the Sword of the Spirit, which is His Word (see Ephesians 6:17), rather than discard His Word as if it is an offence to our own personal will for our life and a stumbling block that we insist must be removed.

The writer to the Hebrew believers says,

"For the word of God is living and active and full of power [making it operative, energizing, and effective]. It is sharper than any two-edged sword, penetrating as far as the division of the soul and spirit [the completeness of a person], and of both joints and marrow [the deepest parts of our nature], exposing and judging the very thoughts and intentions of the heart." – Hebrews 4:12 AMP

Those in the Church, particularly in leadership, must take seriously the precious Holy Word of God which He has entrusted us to read, obey and teach. We cannot mess around with the Word of God and expect to get away with it. On the Day of Judgement, how we have handled and used His Word, and also our personal attitude to what He says, will either end in glory for us or it will be our downfall. The Word will be our judge (see John 12:48). The Sword of the Spirit (the Word of God) will either judge us as true and faithful followers of Christ, or it will pierce us through with gut-wrenching conviction for our rebellion against His Word.

Which would we prefer it to be?

Chapter 4 - Section D

False messiahs; The New World Order & One World Religion; The Rapture, The Second Coming and End of the World Date-Setters; Brother betraying Brother

False messiahs

Followers of Christ ought to know that Jesus is going to return, but what is hard to comprehend is that some are actually being deceived into believing that Jesus has **already** come back! Are these believers reading their Bibles? Have they not read Jesus' warning regarding the appearance of false messiahs prior to His return?

"Then if anyone tells you, 'Look, here is the Messiah,' or 'There he is,' don't believe it. For false messiahs and false prophets will rise up and perform great signs and wonders so as to deceive, if possible, even God's chosen ones. See, I have warned you about this ahead of time." - Matthew 24:23-25

False messiahs are popping up around the world and are drawing in thousands of people who claim to be Christians. These people are longing for Jesus' return, but sadly they have taken their eyes off God's Word. Their desperate longing to see Jesus has caused them to become vulnerable to evil-minded people, whose sole desire is to deceive people by claiming that they are Jesus, to have people follow and worship them, and believe their false teachings.

An Internet search will reveal many of these false messiahs, but here are just a few on the scene today.

Louis Farrakhan

This man claims to be the 'true Jesus', yet his teachings are totally antichrist and blasphemous against the Word of God. You only have to read some of the online articles and listen to some of his 'preaching' videos on YouTube to get an idea of his destructive ideology. We would suggest that you don't listen to them for very long; just enough to understand what can happen to a human being when they are deceived by Satan.

Sergey Anatolyevitch Torop

Also known as Vissarion to his followers, this man leads a cult known as 'The Church of the Last Testament', which is situated in the Taiga forest in Siberia. He looks like the 'Jesus' that the media portray, and he has many followers. He even has his own website, and there are videos of this false messiah on YouTube.

Jose Luis de Jesus Miranda

Founder and leader of 'Growing in Grace International Ministry Inc.', this man claims he is 'the man Jesus'. Bizarrely, he claims to be both Jesus Christ **and** the Antichrist, and has the numbers 666 tattooed on his arm (see Revelation 13:18).

Baha'u'llah

This man has declared himself to be the 'promised One' of all religions, claiming to be several 'messiahs' converging into one person, symbolically.

Other names which you can research for more information:

Jesus of Kitwe, Zambia
Inri Cristo of Brazil
Jesus Matayoshi of Japan
Moses Hlongwane of South Africa
David Shayler of England
Alan John Miller of Australia

End Times Signs and Wonders

On YouTube, there are videos of a magician named 'Dynamo', who is drawing large crowds with his performance of tricks that are in the realms of 'signs and wonders'. Whilst he **does not** claim to be the Messiah, this man uses trickery to 'walk on water', and in one of his tricks, he 'ascends' up into the air in front of the statue of Jesus on the top of Sugarloaf Mountain, in Rio de Janeiro, in front of stunned onlookers.

This magician's tricks may just be the tip of the iceberg; Jesus warned His first disciples that in the 'times of the end', false messiahs and false christs would rise up and perform great signs and wonders to deceive people, even God's chosen ones (see Matthew 24:24 & Mark 13:22). We are seeing these things come to pass in our current generation, and we should heed Jesus' warnings, and not get caught up in believing and following the crowds that flock to these deceptions.

It is one thing, as a follower of Christ, to try to walk on water, like Peter did, when Jesus called him to get out of the boat and walk to Him (see Matthew 14:22-32); Peter was looking to Jesus in faith, to enable him to walk on the water. But it is something very different to take supernatural abilities that belong to Jesus and turn them into 'magic tricks' to draw in crowds and fool them for entertainment purposes. Let's remember that people are paying money to see a man perform tricks based on supernatural events. We would consider this to be an offense against the Holy Spirit.

Brothers and sisters-in-Christ, do not follow anyone who appears in these times performing these biblical signs and wonders when they are only doing them to 'wow' the crowds but have no desire to give the glory to God. Nor follow anyone who is proclaiming that they are the Second Coming of Christ. The Scripture below tells us **exactly** how Jesus will return, and for sure this event has **not** occurred yet.

"After saying this, he was taken up into a cloud while they were watching, and they could no longer see him. As they strained to see him rising into heaven, two white-robed men suddenly stood among them. "Men of Galilee," they said, "why are you standing here staring into heaven? Jesus has been taken from you into heaven, but someday he will return from heaven in the same way you saw him go!" – Acts 1:9-12

The New World Order and One World Religion

The Book of Revelation, Chapters 13 and 17, indicates a time when a new world order and one world religion will be created. Many churches are not teaching the flock about the End Times or Bible prophecy, and as such, vast swathes of the flock have barely any knowledge of future events from God's Word. Many think it is some far-fetched, unrealistic ideology that will never happen. We need to wake up! What is in God's Word is going to be fulfilled at some point.

The Rev Dr Clifford Hill wrote about this in his book, *The Reshaping of Britain – Church and State Since the 1960s: A Personal Reflection*, in a whole chapter relating to the late Archbishop Robert Runcie's very liberal multifaith and New Age views, beliefs, statements and practices during his appointment as Archbishop of Canterbury from 1982 to 1991. We strongly encourage you to read his book.

We only need to do a quick search on the Internet and social media to discover a raft of information concerning the subject of this section. Our own search revealed that it is the Vatican's desire to create a New World Order with a One World Religion as the way forward for the 21st century, for the sake of 'religious unity' and 'world unity and peace'. Meetings have been held, with many world leaders and heads of religious institutions and spiritual organisations in attendance. Very disturbingly, this included many high-profile Christian Church leaders from all the major denominations.

The articles suggest that the meetings hope to persuade these leaders, from all forms of 'faith', to embrace the ideology of this New World Order and One World Religion. With the occasional media reports of these meetings, and the spin that is put on them for the 'peace and security' of the global population, at some point it would then be easy to put their ideology into effect.

Some Internet articles show that there could be a merging of

Christianity and Islam, creating a 'unified' religion called 'Chrislam'. There is a dedicated website about this, www.chrislam.org which states that it is the Islamic-Christian Dialogue Committee. There are many other websites discussing this subject, so it is not something that is imaginary. In fact, there are sites which state that Berlin is to build the first 'Chrislam Church', called 'The House of One', which will be an all-in-one mosque, church and synagogue, where Muslims, Christians and Jews can come together to worship and pray, albeit in separate designated areas. They also have a dedicated website on this, www.house-of-one.org

But how long will it be before the three religions are merged together into the 'unity' of this One World Religion? At the time of writing this (May 9th 2019) the House of One's own website says there are 340 days left until they have their 'Foundation Stone Ceremony'. That takes us to early April 2020. This knowledge should blast us out of our slumber; out of our comfy Christian bubble where everything is all nice and cosy, with idyllic vicarage tea parties on manicured lawns, and summer flower festivals to raise funds for the new church toilet! We don't mean to sound so mocking, but at times the Church appears to be in a state of complete comatose on these issues. This scenario is coming upon the earth, and as followers of Christ, we need to study God's Word on it, keep our eyes and ears alert to the signs of the times on the earth, and remain steadfast to His Word when the pressure intensifies in an effort to get us to compromise and conform for the sake of so-called 'unity'.

The Rapture, The Second Coming & End of the World Date-Setters

Over the past few years the Internet has become awash with End Time 'date-setters', with people proclaiming that the Lord has given them dates and times for the rapture, His Second Coming, and even the end of the world. A search on YouTube will bring up a long list of videos that people have made on this subject. We believe that there are many people who are being given genuine dreams and visions by the Lord regarding these issues in order to wake the Church up. Some are posting them on YouTube or writing books about their experience. The books and videos that would seem more believable are the ones that **do not** set dates for the occurring of these events, but are simply alerting people to be watchful and ready for His appearing, so that we will know when it is 'at the door' (see Matthew 24:33 & Mark 13:29).

The Bible says that in the End Times, people will have dreams and visions (see Joel 2:28-29), and Michele knows this to be true because the Lord plagued her with such dreams for a period of four years, which she mentions in her book *The End of the World and What Jesus Has to Say About It.*

Over the years many believers have felt tossed to-and-fro by the Church's confusion about the rapture. Michele prayed about it one night and asked the Lord to clarify it to her. She had no idea how the Lord would do this, so she just left it with Him. A few days after she had prayed, He gave her a very vivid, all-encompassing dream of the rapture, and as is biblically correct, the Lord **did not** give her a date for its occurrence. She told me that the dream was so real to her that she felt it had actually happened. But when she woke up and found herself still in bed, she was terrified because she thought she had been left behind! It took her a while to realise that the Lord had given her this dream in answer to her prayer. The dream He gave her was simply to reassure her of its reality, and I can assure you that it has held her fast to the faithfulness of His Word, and to do all she can to make sure she is ready for that event. I join with her on this matter. We cannot be complacent.

With the way things are upon the earth in these present times, we are both almost desperate for the Lord to return. We have come across many believers who are sensing something changing in the spiritual realm that is manifesting upon the earth, but sadly much of the Bride of Christ has fallen 'asleep' whilst waiting for The Bridegroom (Jesus) to return for her (see Matthew 25).

But we want to warn readers that Satan can see our desperation for Jesus to return and, as such, Satan has latched on to this and is sowing deception into people's dreams in relation to the rapture, the Second Coming and the end of the world where they are predicting **specific dates** for the occurring of these events.

No Man Knows the Day or the Hour

Jesus has said that no man knows the day or the hour, nor the angels, not even Himself, but only the Father knows (see Matthew 24:36). In view of this, whilst people may be having End Times dreams, and posting them on the Internet and social media, we must ignore and avoid any that **predict dates** for these events, because they are deception and heresy. To say that we have been given a specific date for these things is to exalt ourselves above God. Remember who tried to exalt himself above God? ...Yes, Satan!

Jesus has told us to ignore anyone who predicts specific dates for any of the end times events, as these people are false prophets; liars sent by Satan to deceive and cause believers to fall away in the last days from the true Gospel of Jesus Christ.

Over the years, various names and religious organisations have predicted and proclaimed dates for the rapture, Jesus' return and the end of the world. When those dates have arrived and Jesus has not returned, they just dismiss it as a simple miscalculation, without any explanation for their errors, and then they set a new 'predicted date', and blindly their 'followers' believe them again!

Examples

The following are a few examples of people who have been 'date-setters', and the ones we have mentioned at the end of this list show the disastrous consequences of their deception.

An Internet search will reveal that:

1. In 1843 William Miller predicted that Jesus would return sometime between 1843-1844.

2. In 1876 Charles Taze Russell, founder of the Jehovah's Witnesses, predicted the great day of the Lord would be in 1914. Since then, the Jehovah's Witnesses have predicted many other dates for Jesus' return, all of which have failed.
3. Jack Van Impe has given vague predictions of particular years that the rapture and Second Coming may occur, all of which have failed.
4. Edgar Whisenant, a former NASA engineer and Bible student gave predictions that the rapture would be in 1988, writing books that sold millions of copies. His predictions came and went without fulfilment.
5. Harold Camping predicted the end of the world to be on May 21st 2011. When that failed to happen, he amended it to October 21st 2011.
6. Others who have predicted dates have been J.R. Church and Peter Ruckman.

For a fairly detailed list of the many date-setters that have arisen since the time of Jesus' ascension into heaven, check out the website www.raptureready1.com

Shockingly, some false prophets have even deceived their 'followers' with teaching that they must give up their own life if Jesus fails to return on their predicted date. It must be the height of desperation to end up following one of these charlatans. All the information below is easily accessible to read in the public domain.

1. Jim Jones claimed to be a reincarnation of Jesus and taught a blend of Christianity, socialism and communism to his followers. In 1978, he ordered his 900 followers to commit suicide by drinking a concoction containing cyanide.
2. David Koresh founded The Branch of the Davidians, which stemmed from the Seventh-Day Adventists teachings. He kept 'spiritual wives', some who were under-age. He claimed he was

God, and he and 80 of his followers burned to death in the siege that took place in Waco, Texas in 1993.

3. Marshall Applewhite, another self-proclaimed messiah and the leader of the Heavens Gate sect, organised for his 38 followers to commit suicide in 1997.
4. The Manson Family, created by Charles Manson in the 1960's, had mostly young women followers who believed him to be a reincarnation of Jesus. He provoked his followers to kill people.
5. The Family International was founded by David Brandt Berg in 1968. He endorsed sex with children, resulting in some children born into this cult to later end up killing themselves.
6. The Russian Doomsday Cult was a breakaway movement from the Russian Orthodox Church. In 2007, about 30 members holed themselves up in a cave, and their leader, Pyotr Kuznetsov, told them to stay there as the end of the world was coming in 2008. The members said they would commit suicide if authorities intervened. In the end, 14 people gave up and came out after 6 months, plus 9 more a few months later. Two people died in the cave.
7. The Movement for the Restoration of the Ten Commandments was founded in Uganda in 1989 as a breakaway religious movement from the Roman Catholic Church. They predicted the end of the world to be 31st December 1999. When this didn't happen, they reset it to 17th March 2000 and invited their followers to a big party at a church. A large number of about 530 followers attended, which included many children. The leaders had boarded up all the doors and windows, and once everyone was inside the venue burst into flames, killing them all. Many other bodies were discovered in other compounds across Uganda, belonging to this group. A total of 924 people died at the hands of the cult.

We are seeing the fulfilment of Jesus' warnings of the rise in false messiahs and date-setters. God's Word makes it very clear that no one will know the day or the hour of Jesus' return (see Matthew 25:13). Our part is to **keep watch** for the biblical signs of the approaching end (see Matthew 24) and to exhort each other to make ourselves ready to be taken up in glory to meet the Lord in the air (see 1 Thessalonians 4:17).

Brother betraying Brother

With the explosion of Christianity in non-Christian China, we read on social media of school pupils being forced by teachers to inform them if their parents are Christians and if they hold church activities in their homes. These children are being put into the position of having to betray their own family members, so that the authorities can clamp down on the spread of Christianity. In other countries we hear that authorities will pay family members to betray those who are Christian, with these believing family members then being rounded up and killed. Jesus told us that this, and escalating lawlessness, would come in the times leading up to His return:

"A brother will betray his brother to death, a father will betray his own child, and children will rebel against their parents and cause them to be killed." – Matthew 10:21

"Many false prophets will appear and mislead many. Because lawlessness is increased, the love of most people will grow cold." – Matthew 24:11-12 AMP

In very recent days, we are seeing situations in the United Kingdom where Christian street preachers are being arrested. Christian teachers are being sacked by their Christian employers for openly speaking up against the rising tide of secular teaching that is being taught by Church schools; teaching which directly opposes God's Word. We have heard of other Christian employees and owners of companies who have been targeted by secular people hoping to make a fast buck by attacking their faith on the basis of so-called 'discrimination', making the lives of those Christians a misery for simply upholding their right to live their Christian faith each day at their place of work.

We have recently heard of Cathedral staff calling the police to arrest a Christian for reading the Bible out loud outside the building in the Cathedral grounds! What has it come to when those **within** the Church begin to betray fellow believers in this way, on Christian premises?

And at the time of writing this (July 2019), a case has come to light of a Christian doctor being dismissed after saying he would not refer to any 6ft-tall bearded man as 'Madam'. Instead of the Church supporting him in the court, the Church of England's own 'new' teaching on transgenderism is actually being used by those who sacked him, as evidence against this man's own biblically-sound beliefs!

Andrea Williams, representing The Christian Legal Centre (the sister organisation of Christian Concern) who are acting on behalf of this doctor, said,

'I have spent a lot of time trying to tell Christians, of all denominations, that our public witness to the truth – all aspects of it – is vital... But this week, for the first time, what the Church of England says was used against a Christian in court. For me it was another stark reminder of the damage caused by the Church of England's abandonment of truth.' [11]

When the Church abandons God's word and adopts the beliefs of the world, this is the result. The Church has entered the era of 'brother betraying brother'.

This story can be read on:

https://www.christianconcern.com/our-issues/church-and-state/cofe-teaching-used-as-evidence-against-christian-in-court

Jesus warned us that such treatment would come to those who stand up in His name. He says,

"Blessed [comforted by inner peace and God's love] are those who are persecuted for doing that which is morally right, for theirs is the kingdom of heaven [both now and forever]. Blessed [morally courageous and spiritually alive with life-joy in God's goodness] are you when people insult you and persecute you, and falsely say all kinds of evil things against you because of [your association with] Me. Be glad and exceedingly joyful, for your reward in heaven is great [absolutely inexhaustible]; for in this same way they persecuted the prophets who were before you." – Matthew 5:10-12 AMP

To conclude this whole chapter, as we have seen, a takeover is occurring in our churches, and it is increasing as the days go by. In many churches, the changes have been discussed by the hierarchy for many months in advance, and appointments and ordinations of people into high office positions (who do not meet the biblical criteria) have been agreed long before the congregation have any idea of what is going on behind their backs. By then it is too late for their objections to have any effect. We believe that things are kept hush by those in high office because what is being foisted on the flock is a carefully planned demonic takeover in the House of God. We confidently say this because any church that intends to twist God's Holy Word and create new teaching out of their distortion, (and still call it Christianity), is actually working (knowingly or unknowingly) for the devil and not God. Therefore, those who are involved in this activity are attempting to take over the House of God by deceptive, demonic means. They have no intention of upholding and obeying God's Word; they want to change the Church into an organisation that suits their agenda instead of the will of God.

How are we to respond and treat ministers who come to us trying to impose upon us their false teachings? Let's see what the apostle John has to say:

"Anyone who runs on ahead and does not remain in the doctrine

of Christ [that is, one who is not content with what He taught], does not have God; but the one who continues to remain in the teaching [of Christ does have God], he has both the Father and the Son. ***If anyone comes to you and does not bring this teaching [but diminishes or adds to the doctrine of Christ], do not receive or welcome him into your house, and do not give him a greeting or any encouragement; for the one who gives him a greeting [who encourages him or wishes him success, unwittingly] participates in his evil deeds.***" – 2 John 9-11 AMP (Authors' emphasis)

We mustn't confuse this passage with Jesus' teaching that we are to love our neighbour as ourselves. Indeed, we are to do our best in showing the love of God to those who do not know Christ; we are to bless them and pray that they come to repentance and salvation. But what we have in the above Scripture is a totally different situation. Here John is telling us that **we are to have nothing to do with professing ministers of God who are openly and blatantly rejecting the doctrines of Christ by adding to it or diminishing it**. If we ignore this warning, if we welcome, bless and encourage these imposters in any way whatsoever, then we are participants in their sin.

What a shock this is! I doubt that many in the Church do what John is instructing us to do in this passage, possibly for the simple reason of not wanting to appear unfriendly towards them. But this Scripture is unambiguous in its instruction of how believers are to treat those who are false teachers; wolves in sheep's clothing. We must have the courage to obey this. Such imposters may not like the biblical stand that we take against them, but our integrity and faithfulness to God's Word will stick fast in their conscience. It will be a troubling thorn in their flesh that will constantly goad them, exhorting them to come to repentance. They might repent, but equally they might not; but regardless of whether they respond or not, when God's Word instructs us to have no fellowship with them and offer no greeting or encouragement to them at all, God knows what He is doing and He means what He says. Our obedience is essential, even though we may not understand why we must do something that seems to us to be so un-Christlike. But when Jesus gave people teaching that they did not like or felt uncomfortable with, He remained steadfast to the Word of His Father and simply left them with His powerful, convicting truth ringing in their ears (see Matthew 10:17-27).

Jesus also instructed His disciples to shake the dust off their feet if people they preached to would not listen to or receive their message. The translation below has a powerful ending:

"And if anyone doesn't listen to you and rejects your message, when you leave that house or town, ***shake the dust off your feet as a prophetic act that you will not take their defilement with you.****"* – Matthew 10:14 TPT (Authors' emphasis)

We must stand firm to the Word of God in the face of religious rebellion; we must speak the truth to them and then leave it there. We must not take on board their apostate, deceptive and heretical beliefs or be drawn into their desire to debate, argue, degrade and mock what Scripture says.

The evidence is all around us that the Church is neck-deep in the time of the great falling away from the faith. Outwardly it may appear that the faith of many of these churches is still standing, but inwardly they are in chaos and decay, and will soon collapse like a pack of cards. God will not let these 'lampstands' remain, as the stench of their wicked deception and unrepentant sins will reach the nostrils of God and He will see to it that they are snuffed out.

Whilst all hell appears to be breaking loose in the Church, let us be reassured that a time will come when the thoughts and actions of all who claim to know God, but who wilfully oppose and stand in defiance against the knowledge of His Word, will be destroyed by His divine power.

"For although we live in the natural realm, we don't wage a military campaign employing human weapons, using manipulation

to achieve our aims. Instead, our spiritual weapons are energized with divine power to effectively dismantle the defenses behind which people hide. ***We can demolish every deceptive fantasy that opposes God and break through every arrogant attitude that is raised up in defiance of the true knowledge of God. We capture, like prisoners of war, every thought and insist that it bow in obedience to the Anointed One.***" – 2 Corinthians 10:3-5 TPT (Authors' emphasis)

"And don't forget Sodom and Gomorrah and their neighboring towns, which were ***filled with immorality and every kind of sexual perversion. Those cities were destroyed by fire and serve as a warning of the eternal fire of God's judgment.***" – Jude 7 AMP (Authors' emphasis)

But while these wolves are no longer lurking on the side lines of our churches but are now glaringly visible for all to see, jubilantly promoting all manner of sin as now being acceptable and permittable, turning the sanctuary of the House of God into a place where 'anything goes', let us, the sheep, run from these places and not look back, so that we do not get swept away in their destruction.

Chapter 5

THE DAY OF JUDGEMENT

"Stand in silence in the presence of the Sovereign Lord, for the awesome day of the Lord's judgment is near." – Zephaniah 1:7(a)

The Day of Judgement. These words ought to send shivers down our spine. If we had committed a crime and were now standing in a Court of Law awaiting judgement, then we would most likely be quaking in our boots. But, from a spiritual perspective, when people hear the words 'The Day of Judgement', most unbelievers would laugh and mock, thinking that it is just some apocalyptic story made up by fanatics to scare people. They carry on living their lives without God as if nothing is ever going to happen to upset their life or the plans they have for the future.

In this chapter we will look at what the Bible says concerning The Day of Judgement for everyone. Let's start with the Words of Jesus Himself:

"I tell you... unless you repent [change your old way of thinking, turn from your sinful ways and live changed lives], ***you will all likewise perish.****"* – Luke 13:3 AMP (Authors' emphasis)

Unbelievers

As this book has primarily been written for believers, we will not spend a great deal of time on the issue of what will happen for unbelievers on the Day of Judgement other than to set forth some more of Jesus' own Words on this foreboding, impending event.

Here is what He says:

"Enter through the narrow gate. For wide is the gate and broad and easy to travel is the path that leads the way to destruction and eternal loss, and there are many who enter through it." – Matthew 7:13 AMP

"You are from below, I am from above; you are of this world, I am not of this world. That is why I told you that you will die [unforgiven and condemned] in your sins; for if you do not believe that I am the One [I claim to be], you will die in your sins." – John 8:23-24 AMP

"Whoever rejects Me and refuses to accept My teachings, has one who judges him; the very word that I spoke will judge and condemn him on the last day." – John 12:48 AMP

*"But cowards, **unbelievers**, the corrupt, murderers, the immoral, those who practice witchcraft, idol worshipers, and all liars—their fate is in the fiery lake of burning sulfur."* – Revelation 21:8 (Authors' emphasis)

Below are two more Scriptures from the New Testament writers:

"Be careful that you do not refuse to listen to the One who is speaking. For if the people of Israel did not escape when they refused to listen to Moses, the earthly messenger, we will certainly not escape if we reject the One who speaks to us from heaven!" – Hebrews 12:25

"For the time has come for judgment, and it must begin with God's household. And if judgment begins with us, what terrible fate awaits those who have never obeyed God's Good News?" – 1 Peter 4:17

And one from the Old Testament:

"The LORD of Heaven's Armies says, "The day of judgment is coming, burning like a furnace. On that day the arrogant and the wicked will be burned up like straw. They will be consumed—roots, branches, and all." – Malachi 4:1

If you are an unbeliever, we pray that you will lay down your unbelief and give your life to Jesus Christ to save you. The Day of Judgement is not a joke. It will really happen, and when you come face to face with Jesus, whom you have rejected, you will know that He is real and that He is the Saviour of all who **believe** in Him. But you will be judged as an unbeliever. The above Scriptures confirm what will happen to all who do not believe. Our prayer for you is that you will repent of your sins and turn to Jesus to forgive you and save you, and then follow Him and obey His Word in every area of your life, so that you will have the joy of entering into eternal life with Him forever. We would encourage you to read the *Addendum – Do You know where You're Going to?* which is near the end of this book.

Believers

Now we come to the issue of those who profess to be followers of Christ. Rather disturbingly, many believers have a compromising and complacent attitude concerning the Day of Judgement. They have a mindset that believes that, even as a Christian, they can now just get on with living in this world however they wish, because, in their view, the probability of Jesus returning in their lifetime is about as unlikely as mankind being able to live on Mars. They convince themselves that having given their lives to Christ, they are now safe and don't need to be concerned about His return. This is a very complacent attitude to have.

Then we have the position of many leaders of the Church who are not true shepherds at all, with Jesus describing them as wolves in sheep's clothing. Then finally we have those who are faithful and obedient followers of Christ.

What does God's Word say about the Day of Judgement for each of these types of believers?

Compromising and Complacent Believers

To be a complacent believer is a dangerous position to be in; such a person has given their life to Christ but has become comfortable with their life in the world; they go to church, sing the worship songs and join in the fellowship, but seem to have a somewhat slack attitude to God's Word and their responsibility to obey it. Because they don't have their heads in their Bibles they are easily led into all kinds of other 'spiritual' teaching that they hear. In Jesus' letters to the churches in the Book of Revelation, He told them what He saw that was wrong, and He warned them to repent, or consequences would come. In one of these letters He said,

"I know all that you do, and I know that you are neither frozen in apathy nor fervent with passion. How I wish you were either one or the other! ***But because you are neither cold nor hot, but lukewarm, I am about to spit you from my mouth.*** *"* – Revelation 3:15-16 TPT (Authors' emphasis)

A thorough read of all of Jesus' letters to the churches would do us some good, and will hopefully wake us up out of our slumber, because if Jesus Himself can see our complacency and is trying to warn us to do something about it, if we fail to respond then we are in serious danger of peril.

The Old Testament prophet Amos said,

"You push away every thought of coming disaster, but your actions only bring the day of judgment closer." – Amos 6:3

Paul said to the believers in Rome:

"But because you are stubborn and refuse to turn from your sin, you are storing up terrible punishment for yourself. For a day of anger is coming, when God's righteous judgment will be revealed. *He will judge everyone according to what they have done."* – Romans 2:5-6 (Authors' emphasis)

Paul exhorted the believers to take drastic action in view of the approaching Day:

"The night is almost gone; the day of salvation will soon be here. ***So***

remove your dark deeds like dirty clothes, and put on the shining armor of right living." – Romans 13:12 (Authors' emphasis)

The Living Bible translation renders that verse as follows:

"The night is far gone, the day of his return will soon be here. So quit the evil deeds of darkness and put on the armor of right living, as we who live in the daylight should! ***Be decent and true in everything you do so that all can approve your behavior. Don't spend your time in wild parties and getting drunk or in adultery and lust or fighting or jealousy.***" – Romans 13:12-13 TLB (Authors' emphasis)

As Christians, we are left in this world by God to fulfil His purposes, but we should **not** be so 'in the world' that, by the things we do and the lifestyles that we lead, no one would believe we were a Christian. We are **not** supposed to love the things of this world to the point that we are distracted by them, with worldly events ever drawing us to attend them. If we had an annual look at our diary, what would we find? How much of it would be filled up with the pleasures of this life? Yes, we must take time out for rest and relaxation, but we must discern when these things are becoming a habit or even a craving. When the things of this world are pulling at us and are becoming a temptation that we are struggling to resist, then we need to take note and get off the wide path of the ways of the world that lead to destruction, and back onto the narrow path that leads to life (see Matthew 7:13-14). We cannot play about with our faith, with one foot in the kingdom of God and the other foot in the world.

"No one can serve two masters; for either he will hate the one and love the other, or he will be devoted to the one and despise the other. You cannot serve God and mammon [money, possessions, fame, status, or whatever is valued more than the Lord]." – Matthew 6:24 AMP

In the following parable, Jesus says that followers of the Bridegroom (Jesus) who are not watchful, alert and prepared for His return – meaning that they are living their Christian life in a complacent, compromising, or lukewarm manner, (more like that of the world than of His kingdom) – will not be permitted entry into the kingdom of heaven.

"Then the kingdom of heaven shall be likened to ten virgins who took their lamps and went out to meet the bridegroom. Now five of them were wise, and five were foolish. Those who were foolish took their lamps and took no oil with them, but the wise took oil in their vessels with their lamps. But while the bridegroom was delayed, they all slumbered and slept. "And at midnight a cry was heard: 'Behold, the bridegroom is coming; go out to meet him!' Then all those virgins arose and trimmed their lamps. And the foolish said to the wise, 'Give us some of your oil, for our lamps are going out.' But the wise answered, saying, 'No, lest there should not be enough for us and you; but go rather to those who sell, and buy for yourselves.' And while they went to buy, the bridegroom came, and those who were ready went in with him to the wedding; and the door was shut. "Afterward the other virgins came also, saying, 'Lord, Lord, open to us!' But he answered and said, 'Assuredly, I say to you, I do not know you.' "Watch therefore, for you know neither the day nor the hour in which the Son of Man is coming." – Matthew 25:1-13 NKJV

What a serious warning this is, and if we are living our Christian life like this then we need to wake up, repent and get our lives right with God. Many Christians believe the phrase, "Once saved, always saved". Well, these Words of Jesus clearly indicate that it is possible for a follower of Christ to be living in such a way that they are not ready for His return, and will be told by Him that He does not even know them, and they will not be allowed into the kingdom.

No one who professes to be a follower of Christ should ever want to hear those devastating Words. On the Day of Judgement, many who say they believe in Jesus could find themselves shut out of the kingdom...forever.

Wolves in sheep's clothing

We need to remind ourselves that the Church is the place where the Holy Spirit dwells, and, as such, it should be diligently kept clean, pure and holy. It should not be used to explore and promote teaching that is diametrically opposed to the Word of God. This applies to our church institutions and the many denominations that exist, as well as to ourselves as individuals. God has a warning to all who try to do this:

"Do you not know and understand that you [the church] are the temple of God, and that the Spirit of God dwells [permanently] in you [collectively and individually]? ***If anyone destroys the temple of God [corrupting it with false doctrine], God will destroy the destroyer****; for the temple of God is holy (sacred), and that is what you are."* - 1 Corinthians 3:16-17 AMP (Authors' emphasis)

A terrible judgement awaits those who have crept into the Church through false motives and are destroying the flock with their lies; their twisting of God's Word to suit their own sinful, unrepentant flesh or other unbiblical motives.

They may think they have succeeded in 'getting one over' on God whilst they live in this earthly life, but God is not mocked, and He **will** have the final say. The words of the Old Testament prophets were warnings to the leaders of His chosen people, the Children of Israel, because the leaders had stopped warning the people about their sin. In effect they had stopped keeping watch over the flock. But these words are also prophetic words for the Church today. God's Words are warnings to every generation.

"What sorrow awaits the leaders of my people—the shepherds of my sheep—for they have destroyed and scattered the very ones they were expected to care for," says the LORD. Therefore, this is what the LORD, the God of Israel, says to these shepherds: "Instead of caring for my flock and leading them to safety, you have deserted them and driven them to destruction. Now I will pour out judgment on you for the evil you have done to them." – Jeremiah 23:1-2

"In that day those the LORD has slaughtered will fill the earth from one end to the other. No one will mourn for them or gather up

their bodies to bury them. They will be scattered on the ground like manure. Weep and moan, you evil shepherds! Roll in the dust, you leaders of the flock! The time of your slaughter has arrived; you will fall and shatter like a fragile vase. You will find no place to hide; there will be no way to escape." – Jeremiah 25:33-35

"Then this message came to me from the LORD: "Son of man, prophesy against the shepherds... Give them this message from the Sovereign LORD: What sorrow awaits you shepherds who feed yourselves instead of your flocks. Shouldn't shepherds feed their sheep?" – Ezekiel 34:1-2

"Therefore, you shepherds, hear the word of the LORD: As surely as I live, says the Sovereign LORD, you abandoned my flock and left them to be attacked by every wild animal. And though you were my shepherds, you didn't search for my sheep when they were lost. You took care of yourselves and left the sheep to starve. Therefore, you shepherds, hear the word of the LORD. This is what the Sovereign LORD says: I now consider these shepherds my enemies, and I will hold them responsible for what has happened to my flock. I will take away their right to feed the flock, and I will stop them from feeding themselves." – Ezekiel 34:7-10(a)

"Therefore, this is what the Sovereign LORD says: I will surely judge between the fat sheep and the scrawny sheep. For you fat sheep pushed and butted and crowded my sick and hungry flock until you scattered them to distant lands. So I will rescue my flock, and they will no longer be abused." – Ezekiel 34:20-22(a)

"Gather before judgment begins, before your time to repent is blown away like chaff. Act now, before the fierce fury of the LORD falls and the terrible day of the LORD's anger begins." – Zephaniah 2:2

In the New Testament, Jesus warns:

"Whoever rejects Me and refuses to accept My teachings, has one who judges him; the very word that I spoke will judge and condemn him on the last day." – John 12:48 AMP

The apostle Paul says,

"For [God does not overlook sin and] the wrath of God is revealed from heaven against ***all ungodliness and unrighteousness of men who in their wickedness suppress and stifle the truth,..*** *"* – Romans 1:18 AMP (Authors' emphasis)

"But because you are stubborn and refuse to turn from your sin, you are storing up terrible punishment for yourself. For a day of anger is coming, when God's righteous judgment will be revealed. He will judge everyone according to what they have done." – Romans 2:5-6

All of this is so serious. Our prayer is that many who are in the category of wolves in sheep's clothing, parading around in the Church as ministers of God, will be overcome by the Holy Spirit, bringing upon them a crushing conviction of their sin so that they can confess and repent, receive God's forgiveness, and start afresh. It is not too late. God does not want any to perish (see 2 Peter 3:9). But one day it will be too late; the time for repentance will be over and we will reap what we have sown in this life.

"Do not be deceived, God is not mocked [He will not allow Himself to be ridiculed, nor treated with contempt nor allow His precepts to be scornfully set aside]*; for whatever a man sows, this and this only is what he will reap.* ***For the one who sows to his flesh [his sinful capacity, his worldliness, his disgraceful impulses] will reap from the flesh ruin and destruction****, but the one who sows to the Spirit will from the Spirit reap eternal life."* – Galatians 6:7-8 AMP (Authors' emphasis)

Added to what Paul is saying in that passage, Ryle has some sobering words to say about the convicting Words of Jesus, "Except you repent, you will all likewise perish!" (see Luke 13:3).

'Oh, think what dreadful words are these! Who can measure out the full amount of what they contain? "Shall perish!" Perish in body – perish in soul – perish miserably at last in hell! I dare not attempt to paint the horrors of that thought. The worm that never dies, the fire

that is not quenched, the blackness of darkness forever, the hopeless prison, the bottomless pit, the lake that burns with fire and brimstone – all, all are but feeble emblems of the reality of hell. And to this hell all impenitent people are daily travelling! Yes – from churches and chapels, from rich men's mansions and poor men's cottages, from the midst of knowledge, wealth, and respectability – all who will not repent are certainly travelling towards hell. "Except you repent, you shall all perish!"' [1]

It cannot be spelt out any clearer. Both Jesus' and Ryle's words ought to stir up every Christian, both the shepherds and the sheep, to examine their life, wake up and repent as a matter of urgency.

And just to confirm the matter, Jesus has some fiery Words to say about the drastic action we need to take concerning sin and the serious issue of deceiving the flock:

"But whoever causes one of these little ones who believe and trust in Me to stumble [that is, to sin or lose faith], it would be better for him if a heavy millstone [one requiring a donkey's strength to turn it] were hung around his neck and he were thrown into the sea. If your hand causes you to stumble and sin, cut it off [that is, remove yourself from the source of temptation]! It is better for you to enter life crippled, than to have two hands and go into hell, into the unquenchable fire, [where THEIR WORM DOES NOT DIE, AND THE FIRE IS NOT PUT OUT.] If your foot causes you to stumble and sin, cut it off [that is, remove yourself from the source of temptation]! It would be better for you to enter life lame than to have two feet and be thrown into hell [where THEIR WORM DOES NOT DIE, AND THE FIRE IS NOT PUT OUT.] If your eye causes you to stumble and sin, throw it out [that is, remove yourself from the source of temptation]! It would be better for you to enter the kingdom of God with one eye, than to have two eyes and be thrown into hell, where THEIR WORM [that feeds on the dead] DOES NOT DIE, AND THE FIRE IS NOT PUT OUT."
– Mark 9:42-48 AMP

Note that three times Jesus uses the Words, "where their worm does not die, and the fire is not put out". If you are a shepherd who has crept into the Church with false motives and are deceiving the flock with teachings that are contrary to God's Word, we cannot urge you strongly enough to heed Jesus' warning in the above passage. Jesus is not joking…

Faithful and obedient Believers

Believers (whether shepherds or sheep) who live in a repentant way and are obedient to God's Word need not fear the Day of Judgement. God has prepared a place for us in the kingdom of heaven and He is waiting to receive us (see John 14:1-3). As we daily live our lives in Christ doing our best to be about our Father's business, and living in such a way that all that we do brings glory to Him and not grief, then we can have confidence that we will be able to stand before His throne where we will hear Him say these wonderful Words, *"Well done, good and faithful servant! You have been faithful with a few things; I will put you in charge of many things. Come and share your master's happiness!"* (Matthew 25:23 NIV) and *"Come, you who are blessed by my Father; take your inheritance, the kingdom prepared for you since the creation of the world."* (Matthew 25:34 NIV).

Let us live each day longing to be with Him in glory, being alert and ever watchful for the day when we are called up to be with Him. The knowledge of this should fill us with joyful anticipation, and ought to be lodged in the forefront of our minds as we witness signs on the earth that fulfil End Times prophecy. God's Word says that faithful followers of Christ **are not appointed to wrath**, but to obtain salvation (see 1 Thessalonians 5:9) so we need have no fear of the Day of Judgement. We will be clothed in a robe of righteousness, and we will be welcomed into the kingdom, as the following Scripture passage confirms:

"Let us rejoice and shout for joy! Let us give Him glory and honor, for the marriage of the Lamb has come [at last] and ***His bride (the***

redeemed) has prepared herself. *" She has been permitted to dress in fine linen, dazzling white and clean—**for the fine linen signifies the righteous acts of the saints [the ethical conduct, personal integrity, moral courage, and godly character of believers].*** *"* - Revelation 19:7-8 AMP (Authors' emphasis)

Let's have a look at some more passages that will fill us with hope for what lies ahead for all who are truly God's faithful children.

"Once you were alienated from God and were enemies in your minds because of your evil behavior. ***But now he has reconciled you by Christ's physical body through death to present you holy in his sight, without blemish and free from accusation— if you continue in your faith, established and firm, and do not move from the hope held out in the gospel.*** *"* - Colossians 1:21-23(a) NIV (Authors' emphasis)

"When is all this going to happen? I really don't need to say anything about that, dear brothers, for you know perfectly well that no one knows. That day of the Lord will come unexpectedly, like a thief in the night. When people are saying, "All is well; everything is quiet and peaceful"—then, all of a sudden, disaster will fall upon them as suddenly as a woman's birth pains begin when her child is born. And these people will not be able to get away anywhere—there will be no place to hide. ***But, dear brothers, you are not in the dark about these things, and you won't be surprised as by a thief when that day of the Lord comes. For you are all children of the light and of the day, and do not belong to darkness and night. So be on your guard, not asleep like the others. Watch for his return and stay sober. Night is the time for sleep and the time when people get drunk. But let us who live in the light keep sober, protected by the armor of faith and love, and wearing as our helmet the happy hope of salvation. For God has not chosen to pour out his anger upon us but to save us through our Lord Jesus Christ; he died for us so that we can live with him forever, whether we are dead or alive at the time of his return. So encourage each***

other to build each other up, just as you are already doing. *"* – 1 Thessalonians 5:1-11 TLB (Authors' emphasis)

"I have fought the good fight, I have finished the race, I have kept the faith. ***Now there is in store for me the crown of righteousness, which the Lord, the righteous Judge, will award to me on that day—and not only to me, but also to all who have longed for his appearing.*** *"* – 2 Timothy 4:7-8 NIV (Authors' emphasis)

"But he has appeared once for all at the culmination of the ages to do away with sin by the sacrifice of himself. Just as people are destined to die once, and after that to face judgment, so Christ was sacrificed once to take away the sins of many; and he will appear a second time, not to bear sin, ***but to bring salvation to those who are waiting for him.*** *"* – Hebrews 9:26b -28 NIV (Authors' emphasis)

"Blessed is the one who perseveres under trial because, having stood the test, ***that person will receive the crown of life that the Lord has promised to those who love him.*** *"* – James 1:12 NIV (Authors' emphasis)

"Praise be to the God and Father of our Lord Jesus Christ! In his great mercy ***he has given us new birth into a living hope through the resurrection of Jesus Christ from the dead, and into an inheritance that can never perish, spoil or fade. This inheritance is kept in heaven for you, who through faith are shielded by God's power until the coming of the salvation that is ready to be revealed in the last time. In all this you greatly rejoice,*** *though now for a little while you may have had to suffer grief in all kinds of trials. These have come so that the proven genuineness of your faith—of greater worth than gold, which perishes even though refined by fire—may result in praise, glory and honor when Jesus Christ is revealed.* ***Though you have not seen him, you love him; and even though you do not see him now, you believe in him and are filled with an inexpressible and glorious joy, for you are receiving the end result of your faith, the salvation of your souls.*** *"* – 1 Peter 1:3-9 NIV (Authors' emphasis)

"Therefore, my brothers and sisters, make every effort to confirm your calling and election. For if you do these things, you will never stumble, ***and you will receive a rich welcome into the eternal kingdom of our Lord and Savior Jesus Christ.****"* – 2 Peter 1:10-11 NIV (Authors' emphasis)

"Dear friends, now we are children of God, and what we will be has not yet been made known. But we know that ***when Christ appears, we shall be like him, for we shall see him as he is. All who have this hope in him purify themselves,*** *just as he is pure."* – 1 John 3:2-3 NIV (Authors' emphasis)

"All who are victorious will be clothed in white. I will never erase their names from the Book of Life, but I will announce before my Father and his angels that they are mine." – Revelation 3:5 (Authors' emphasis)

Oh, what incredible blessings await all who are faithful and obedient believers! These are God's promises to us, so let us daily fix our eyes on eternity whilst we are called to live our life on this earth to fulfil His purposes.

God's 'Day of Judgement' view of His whole Church

The Church is full of a variety of people who profess to follow Christ, but sadly many are not willing to repent of their sin, yet they still attend church services and profess to be Christians. In the following verse, Jesus makes it very plain what will happen to those throughout His whole Church who are unrepentant.

"His winnowing fork is in His hand, and He will thoroughly clear out His threshing floor; and ***He will gather His wheat (believers) into His barn (kingdom), but He will burn up the chaff (the unrepentant) with unquenchable fire.****"* – Matthew 3:12 AMP (Authors' emphasis)

In one whole parable Jesus reveals His 'Day of Judgement' view of the Church, as we will see below:

The Parable of the Weeds and the Wheat

In this parable, Jesus is referring to the 'enemy' planting weeds amongst the fields of wheat. We can take this as a direct message for today's lukewarm, complacent and compromising churches and their leaders. We can interpret the 'enemy' as being Satan, and the 'weeds' as being Satan's workers. His workers are not just unbelievers and devil worshippers; Satan's workers include people in the Church who **profess** to be believers whom he is using to carry out his schemes, whether they are aware of it or not. Jesus said to one of His closest disciples (Peter), "Get behind me Satan!" Why did Jesus say this to one of His followers? Because Peter, at that moment, had his mind not on the things of God but on the things of 'man' (see Matthew 16:23 AMP). So, we believe that the 'weeds' also include church leaders who are preaching and teaching false gospels, since they too have their minds set not on believing and obeying the whole Word of God but, alas, on promoting the unbiblical things of 'man'; of the flesh and of this ungodly world. The 'wheat' refers to the faithful and obedient followers of Christ, and the 'field' as being the Church as a whole.

Here is the parable:

"Jesus gave them another parable [to consider], saying, "The kingdom of heaven is like a man who sowed ***good seed in his field.*** *But while his men were sleeping,* ***his enemy came and sowed weeds [resembling wheat] among the wheat****, and went away. So when the plants sprouted and formed grain, the weeds appeared also. The servants of the owner came to him and said, 'Sir, did you not sow good seed in your field? Then how does it have weeds in it?' He replied to them, 'An enemy has done this.' The servants asked him, 'Then do you want us to go and pull them out?' But he said, 'No; because as you pull out the weeds, you may uproot the wheat with them. Let them grow together until the harvest; and* ***at harvest time I will tell the reapers, "First gather the weeds and tie them in bundles to be burned; but gather the wheat into my barn.*** *"'""* – Matthew 13: 24-30 AMP (Authors' emphasis)

It is clear in this passage that Satan's false leaders (the weeds) will continue to rise up in the Church (the field) right up until the final harvest. The Lord will then separate the evil weeds from the good wheat, and He will burn the weeds (in the furnace of fire – see Matthew 13:40-42 KJV). The wheat He will gather into His barn (kingdom of heaven).

Ryle also has something to say about the above parable and the reality of false leaders remaining in the Church until the final harvest:

'The present mixed state of things is not to be for ever. The wheat and tares are divided at last. The Lord Jesus shall send forth his angels in the day of his second advent. Those mighty reapers shall make no mistake. They shall discern with unerring judgement between the righteous and the wicked and place everyone in his own lot. The worldly, the ungodly, the careless and the unconverted shall be cast into a furnace of fire and receive shame and everlasting contempt.

Let the ungodly man tremble when he reads this parable. Let him see in its fearful language his own certain doom unless he repents and is converted. Let him know that he is sowing misery for himself if he goes on still in neglect of God. Let him reflect that his end will be to be gathered among the bundles of tares and be burned. Surely such a prospect ought to make a man think!' [2]

Whilst this parable says that the weeds will grow amongst the wheat, we should not see this as an instruction for the sheep to remain under their false teaching when, as we have seen throughout this book, God's Word has already told us to flee from them. We each, individually, have the responsibility to make sure that we are under godly authority and listening to sound biblical teaching. So, when we become aware that a minister of Satan is over us, we must flee, or we will be swallowed up in their deception.

We have included Jesus' parable and Ryle's warning as a 'wake up' call to all church leaders who are teaching, preaching and living a liberal or progressive gospel. A liberal gospel is not **the** Gospel. We pray that this warning will cause deep concern in the hearts, souls and spirits of all who are leading and overseeing our churches. The eternal destiny of ourselves and our flock is at stake.

To conclude this chapter, whichever category above that we find ourselves in, the Day of Judgement is coming. For some, God will reward them with everything they have eagerly and patiently longed for, and much more. But for many, that fearful Day will bring upon them all that they have mockingly scoffed and sneered at. Each one of us will reap what we have sown, whether for good or for evil. None of us will escape this divine appointment at the Throne of God, to whom we must give account. The Lord sees and knows everything about us and the lives we are living. Nothing is hidden from Him. With everything that we desire to say and do, we should take a long hard look at our Christian lives and ask ourselves this serious question: "If Jesus Himself were to appear right next to me, what would He think and feel about what I am saying and doing? Is my daily conduct in my thoughts, words and actions, honouring to Him, or does my life display the marks of someone who is a religious hypocrite; someone who outwardly looks like the 'real deal' but inwardly is a 'whitewashed tomb'?"

"Nothing in all creation is hidden from God's sight. Everything is uncovered and laid bare before the eyes of him to whom we must give account." – Hebrews 4:13 NIV

Once we have asked this deeply probing question of ourselves, if we don't like what the Lord is revealing to us about any aspect of our daily lives and the conduct that we so easily dismiss or condone, then we must respond to Him humbly and repentantly, with a broken and contrite heart. If we do this, He will forgive us and restore us (see 1 John 1:9). But if we fail to do this, and continue to **wilfully oppose God**, choosing to carry on in our sin, then judgement awaits us.

"Dear friends, if we deliberately continue sinning after we have received knowledge of the truth, there is no longer any sacrifice that

will cover these sins. There is only the terrible expectation of God's judgment and the raging fire that will consume his enemies." – Hebrews 10:26-27

And just to drive the truth home even further, The Amplified Bible, Classic Edition translation of this passage leaves us without any doubt:

"For if we go on deliberately and willingly sinning after once acquiring the knowledge of the Truth, there is no longer any sacrifice left to atone for [our] sins [no further offering to which to look forward]. ***[There is nothing left for us then] but a kind of awful and fearful prospect and expectation of divine judgment and the fury of burning wrath and indignation which will consume those who put themselves in opposition [to God]."*** (Authors' emphasis)

EPILOGUE

The Sound of the Trumpet – But are we Listening?

"Set the trumpet to your lips [announcing impending judgment]! Like a [great] vulture the enemy comes against the house of the LORD, Because they have broken My covenant and transgressed and rebelled against My law." – Hosea 8:1 AMP

"When the ram's horn blows a warning, shouldn't the people be alarmed?" – Amos 3:6(a)

"He heard the sound of the trumpet but did not take warning; his blood shall be on himself. But if he had taken warning, he would have saved his life." – Ezekiel 33:5 AMP

"This is what the LORD says: "Stop at the crossroads and look around. Ask for the old, godly way, and walk in it. Travel its path, and you will find rest for your souls. But you reply, 'No, that's not the road we want!' ***I posted watchmen over you who said, 'Listen for the sound of the alarm.' But you replied, 'No! We won't pay attention!'*** – Jeremiah 6:16-17 (Authors' emphasis)

Followers of Christ know that heretical teaching in the Church is nothing new. It has been an issue from the moment that the Church was first born, on the Day of Pentecost, after Jesus had ascended into heaven.

However, what we are now witnessing happening within the Church, in many denominations, and at such a rapid pace, must surely indicate to us that we are fast approaching the time of Christ's return. Jesus Himself warned us that these things would escalate as we see the Day approaching! (see Matthew 24:3-26). If Jesus said it, then we had better believe it.

But one of the things that troubles us greatly is that many followers of Christ are living their lives chasing after the next so-called 'Christian' event where they can get their next spiritual 'quick fix'; much of it now being a deception. They don't realise that what they are hankering after is a deception. Their false shepherds have disguised their false teaching so well, using God's Word in distorted ways to entice people into believing their lies. If a preacher says that something is 'okay' for believers to do, instead of checking what they are hearing with what God's Word **actually** says, sadly many believers suck up the heresies that these wolves promulgate.

It is not as if God has not given His children enough teaching about obeying His Word, and enough warnings concerning the consequences of disobedience and rebellion. He has sent prophet after prophet to warn and wake up His people to repent of their sin, and He has even sent His own Son Jesus Christ with the same message, offering them **The Way** of salvation; yet they killed the prophets, and they crucified The Saviour. Many once biblically-sound churches are giving way to worldly influences and are now arrogantly rejecting the 'sound of the trumpet' – the words of godly warning being given to them by those who have the courage to stand up for the uncompromising truth of God's Word.

God gave a message to the prophet Hosea about what His chosen people - the nation of Israel - were saying, and the mocking attitude that they had towards those whom God sent to watch over and guard them. These words equally apply to the Church.

God's people were saying,

"The prophets are crazy"; "The inspired men are mad." *Yes, so they mock, for the nation is weighted with sin and shows only hatred for those who love God.* ***I appointed the prophets to guard my people, but the people have blocked them at every turn and***

publicly declared their hatred, even in the Temple of the Lord. The things my people do are...depraved... *The Lord does not forget. He will surely punish them."* – Hosea 9:7(b)-9 TLB (Authors' emphasis)

In his book, *The Last Hour – An Israeli Insider Looks at the End Times*, the author, Amir Tsarfati says the following about God's purpose of His prophets, and compares this to the deception of prophets in the Church today:

'Who would ever want to be a prophet? First of all, God often asked them to do very strange things. In order to prove a point, God might have a prophet lie on one side for a year, and then flip over to the other side. God could tell a prophet to cook his food on human dung, walk around naked for three years or marry a prostitute. Not a very glamorous calling. Second, prophets were hated by their people. Rarely were they listened to. More often than not, they were ridiculed, beaten and killed. To step into the role of prophet took a true call from God.

Today, the opposite is often true; how easy it is to be honored and held in high esteem! Many measure the worth of a prophet in book sales and television ratings instead of the quality of the prophecy. Prophets themselves may play on fame and flash and fear, and their greatest asset can be image. Like using a screwdriver handle to pound in a nail, such men and women misuse Scripture to bolster their lies rather than to discover truth...

People practically worship them when they step off the plane. They are driven in the finest cars and stay at the finest hotels. Thousands come to hear what they say. Even when their predictions do not come to pass, they are invited back to the next year's conference. Where are the people who will stand up and say, "No! You are a false prophet!"?' [1]

Not only are shepherds rising up in the Church who are actually wolves in sheep's clothing, but so are many of today's so-called prophets, and we must steer clear of them too.

It is a shocking fact that false shepherds and leaders in many areas of ministry are now accepting, affirming and condoning people's sins like never before, and the sheep are lapping it up, desperate to be able to carry on with the lifestyles of their fallen nature and not have to 'crucify the flesh'. Indeed, in reality it is much easier to our human nature to remain as we are and merely **hope** that God will understand our situation and be merciful to us on the Day of Judgement, than it is to crucify our flesh and obey God's Word, day in and day out during our life on earth, even though doing the latter will give us absolute **assurance** of our salvation rather than some vague sort of 'hope'.

To confirm that we need to crucify our flesh, Paul says to Timothy:

*"But God's truth stands firm like a foundation stone with this inscription: "The Lord knows those who are his," and "**All who belong to the Lord must turn away from evil.**"* – 2 Timothy 2:19 (Authors' emphasis)

And Paul says to the believers in Thessalonica:

*"**Finally, believers, we ask and admonish you in the Lord Jesus, that you follow the instruction that you received from us about how you ought to walk and please God** (just as you are actually doing) and that you excel even more and more [pursuing a life of purpose and living in a way that expresses gratitude to God for your salvation]. For you know what commandments and precepts we gave you by the authority of the Lord Jesus. **For this is the will of God, that you be sanctified [separated and set apart from sin]: that you abstain and back away from sexual immorality; that each of you know how to control his own body in holiness and honor [being available for God's purpose and separated from things profane], not [to be used] in lustful passion,** like the Gentiles who do not know God and are ignorant of His will;"* – 1 Thessalonians 4:1-5 AMP (Authors' emphasis)

It seems that many people who profess to be followers of Christ no longer want to be the diligent, faithful and obedient 'Christian soldiers' that our forefathers were; rather, they are now wanting to create a new kind of Christianity that allows them to not have to turn away from sin and evil. They would rather change the Word of God, re-thinking it, reinterpreting it or redefining it in order to justify their perceived 'right' to have 'permission' to remain as they are - in their sinful, unconverted and unregenerate selves - thereby easing their conscience and thus having a much 'easier life'. Being permitted by the Church to live as **we** please may seem easier this side of the grave, but our lives in Christ whilst on this earth are meant to be lived in ways that glorify Him, **not** trample His name in the muck of a culture that aligns itself with that of Sodom and Gomorrah.

No matter what we or our shepherds may now think about God's Word, God means what He says, and His Word is **not** going to change just because we demand that it should!

A Dream

In 2008, Michele had a very vivid dream, and she shares it with you in her own words below:

"It was a very powerful dream, causing me immense grief, and it is one which I will never forget. I understood what the dream was revealing, but at that time I could not see why God was showing it to me, as nothing seemed to be occurring in the Church that caused me any great concern. All seemed to be well in the Church as far as I could tell. However, as the years have passed since this dream was given to me by the Lord, I have now seen what was revealed to me unfolding in front of my eyes on an escalating scale, and my heart is breaking that this is happening.

In the dream I saw a huge wooden cross standing on a hill. Nailed to the cross was every single page of the Bible; each page nailed separately. One by one, people who claimed to be Christians walked up to the cross and began to rip off pages of the Bible. It began slowly at first, with just the odd page here and there fluttering to the ground as people threw away parts of the Word of God that they didn't like or agree with. As the pages of the Bible were torn off, the place where each page had been nailed to the cross revealed a tiny part of the beaten and battered body of Jesus Christ.

But then the steady trickle of Christians walking up to the cross turned into a heaving mass, and the rate at which the pages of the Bible were being ripped off the cross turned into a possessed frenzy filled with indescribable anger and hatred. Every single page of the Word of God was literally being torn from the cross, until the ground around the cross was completely covered in the pages. My eyes then looked up, and there on the cross, previously hidden by the pages that had once been there, was the entire mutilated body of our crucified Saviour, in horrific detail for all to see. But the people just looked at Jesus, and without any emotion, each person turned and walked away.

All of a sudden, I began to realise that what these so-called believers were doing was tearing off the flesh of Jesus, as He is the **Word** of God **made flesh** (see John Chapter 1). In the dream, I began to shake and weep in great sobs of grief as I witnessed the evil of those who professed to be believers ripping the Word of God (Jesus' body) to shreds. They were not content until they had torn every page of the Bible off the cross."

This was the end of the dream. It was a horrifying experience and more like a vivid vision, but its manifestation into real life is even more horrifying to me. I knew God had given me the dream for a reason, but I cannot begin to put into words how I feel as I witness, on a daily basis, the fulfilment of this dream. We are literally seeing believers demanding to remove what God's Word says, or reinterpret it or redefine it, because **they do not like** what He says. Rather than obey His Word, they are tearing it to shreds and discarding it with an almost venomous hatred.

I feel certain that now that this dream is being manifested, what I saw in the dream will not stop until the Church seems satisfied that it has removed enough of God's Word to make them feel 'comfortable' in the lifestyles that they refuse to repent of. I believe that if many of our shepherds had their way, every single page of God's Word would be ripped out of their Bibles because most of Jesus' teachings, and the writings of the apostles, as well as the prophets, command them to confess their sins and to repent, and warns them of the wrath of God that will come upon all who reject and disobey His Word.

Incidentally, this dream occurred about one year prior to another occurrence where the Lord began to wake me up to what was going on in His Church, from His perspective. In 2009, He gave me these powerful words, "Wake Up Church", which resulted in the writing of my first book *Come on Church! Wake Up! Sin Within the Church and What Jesus has to Say About It*. The dream, and then the writing of that book, has made everything fall into place and make sense.

The Future

With major End Times signs occurring every single day on an unprecedented scale at the same time as many denominations of the Church falling headlong into deep deception and heresy, this cannot be a 'coincidence'. What is happening upon the earth is in direct relation and proportion to the staggering apostasy occurring in the Church. This earth is suffering because of the sins of God's people.

"The earth suffers for the sins of its people, for they have twisted God's instructions, violated his laws, and broken his everlasting covenant." – Isaiah 24:5

Now that the Church has opened the floodgates, what we are seeing will continue until the day of Christ's return. No follower of Christ should want to be caught up in this mess, and risk being spewed out of Jesus' mouth at His appearing (see Revelation 3:16).

Fellow believers; open your eyes and really **see** and discern what is happening! It is not your imagination; it is really happening in the Church right now, and it is **not** going to stop. Jesus has warned us that it will happen, and will continue right up until the end.

We have written this book to alert you to some of the things that are happening under the watch of those who profess to be God's shepherds over His flock. What we have shared is merely the tip of the iceberg. As each day goes by, more and more things are coming to the fore, being presented as 'reasons' to overturn and forsake God's Word. The trickle is fast becoming a flood, and we simply cannot keep up with cataloguing it all to present in this book as it would end up twice the size! We would encourage you to keep alert to the escalating apostasy, deception and heresy in the Church by watching some of the many hundreds of videos posted by *Anglican Unscripted* on their YouTube channel *AnglicanTV Ministries* and by visiting their website *www.anglican.ink*

Yet even though the eyes of many sheep are now being opened to what is going on, those who promote the vast arrays of anti-biblical teaching **still** insist on retaining the title of being God's Church. Any church that rebels against God's Word is no longer a part of the Church that was born on the Day of Pentecost; their anti-biblical views and beliefs catapult them into belonging to the 'church of Satan', and unless they repent and turn back to obedience to God's Word, there will be no escape for them on the Day of God's Judgement. But whilst this demonic takeover is happening in the Church in our times, let us remember that ultimately the gates of hell will never prevail against it (see Matthew 16:18). It might seem as though the demonic realm is winning the battle, but at the end of the day, we feel sure that all that is happening is for the purpose of shaking up the Church and separating out the wheat from the chaff; revealing those who are the true and faithful followers of Christ from those who are fake.

Hill says, *'Clearly, we are living in extraordinary days when all the nations and great institutions are being shaken. God is not only looking for individuals to act as watchmen, but for a community of believers who will be his witnesses to the nations, and declare his truth in a generation of fake news, lies and deception. Ideally, the church should be this community of believers. But in so many ways the churches have become institutions after the pattern of the world, and this is especially so in Britain...'* [2]

God will not have a Church that is full of sin and evil, so He will do whatever is necessary to draw His faithful sheep out of the stinking mess. The warning sound of the trumpet is being heard throughout the Church, to wake up and flee from the wickedness of wolves in sheep's clothing. **Do not ignore it**...your eternal destiny depends on it.

Both Michele and I agree with the apostle Paul concerning his all-consuming desire to warn and teach the believers at Colossae. We likewise do this out of a deep love for our fellow believers today, and ultimately to obey God:

"We proclaim Him, ***warning and instructing everyone in all wisdom [that is, with comprehensive insight into the word and purposes of God]****, so that we may present every person complete in Christ [mature, fully trained, and perfect in Him—the Anointed].* ***For this I labor [often to the point of exhaustion], striving with His power and energy,*** *which so greatly works within me."* – Colossians 1:28-29 AMP (Authors' emphasis)

When God's Word says we must warn the sheep of the advancement of the wolves and to flee from them, then we must do exactly that. The sheep may not like the upheaval, but God's command to warn the sheep is the equivalent of being given 'Holy Orders'. Out of our reverential fear of the Lord, we feel compelled to obey Him. If you know that those who lead your church are liberal in their views of Scripture, or you sense that they are compromising and diluting the Word of God in their preaching, teaching, programmes and actions, we urge you to leave and find a church that actually believes what the Bible says, and faithfully preaches and obeys it. Even though much of the mainstream Church seems to be happily throwing itself into apostasy, let us be encouraged that there are also many churches that **are** standing their ground in obedience to God's Word, shining like little beacons of light on the hilltops, casting the light of Christ to all who will see the light and follow it.

Whilst we wait for the return of our Lord and Saviour Jesus Christ, let us heed some final words of one who has walked the path of faith and is now among the great crowd of witnesses in heaven, willing us on to make ourselves ready for that Day that shall come like a thief in the night (see 1 Thessalonians 5:2).

Ryle urges us, whilst we live our daily lives on earth:

'I want to disqualify no man for usefulness upon earth. I require no man to become a hermit, and cease to serve his generation. I call on no man to leave his lawful calling, and neglect his earthly affairs. But I do call on every one to live like one who expects Christ to return: to live soberly, righteously and godly in this present world; to live like a pilgrim and a stranger, ever looking unto Jesus; to live like a good servant, with his loins girded, and his lamp burning; to live like one whose treasure is in heaven, with his heart packed up and ready to be gone. This is readiness. This is preparation. And is this too much to ask? I say unhesitatingly that it is not. Now, reader, are you ready in this way?' [3]

Indeed, are we ready like this? Is the Church ready like this? All the evidence would clearly indicate that huge swathes of it are far from ready. Many church leaders simply say that all that is happening in the Church of the 21st Century is that the Lord is doing a 'new thing' to bring people in by becoming 'relevant' to the world in which we live. Our final word for this book is, yes God **might** do new things, but only ever in line with what His already written Word says. What God **won't** do is overturn His Word, redefine it or rewrite it to suit the wishes and desires of those who say they 'know God' but refuse to obey His Word. It is the discontent in the hearts of professing believers that causes them to want to create new things in Christianity to please their flesh, when what is actually needed in the Church in these closing days, before Jesus returns, is repentance...on a **grand** scale.

We close this book with some final Words from our Lord and Saviour, Jesus Christ.

"Repent [change your inner self—your old way of thinking, regret past sins, ***live your life in a way that proves repentance****; seek God's purpose for your life],* ***for the kingdom of heaven is at hand****."* – Matthew 4:17 AMP (Authors' emphasis)

"So you, too, must ***keep watch! For you don't know what day your Lord is coming.****"* – Matthew 24:42; 25:13; Mark 13:35 (Authors' emphasis)

"Behold, I (Jesus) am coming quickly, and My reward is with Me, to give to each one according to the merit of his deeds (earthly works, faithfulness)." – Revelation 22:12 AMP

"Blessed (happy, prosperous, to be admired) are those who wash their robes [in the blood of Christ by believing and trusting in Him—the righteous who do His commandments], so that they may have the right to the tree of life, and may enter by the gates into the city." – Revelation 22:14 AMP

*"****Be prepared—all dressed and ready****— for your Lord's return from the wedding feast. Then you will be ready to open the door and let him in the moment he arrives and knocks.* ***There will be great joy for those who are ready and waiting for his return. He himself will seat them and put on a waiter's uniform and serve them as they sit and eat!*** *He may come at nine o'clock at night—or even at midnight.* ***But whenever he comes, there will be joy for his servants who are ready!*** *Everyone would be ready for him if they knew the exact hour*

of his return—just as they would be ready for a thief if they knew when he was coming. ***So be ready all the time. For I, the Messiah, will come when least expected.***" – Luke 12:35-40 TLB (Authors' emphasis)

"*Yes, I am coming quickly.*" – Revelation 22:20(b) AMP

Amen. Come, Lord Jesus.

ADDENDUM

Do You know where You're Going to?

We referred to this Addendum in Chapter 5, under the sub-heading **'Unbelievers'**, and we have written it to show all unbelievers the inescapable reason why they need to turn to Jesus Christ to be saved; the critical point of this being to reveal the eternal destiny of those who reject God, but at the same time showing them the way of escape.

In the Beginning

To know why this is essential to all of humanity, we need to go right back to the beginning of creation to find out what happened to the first created humans; Adam and Eve (see Genesis Chapters 1 to 4). When God created them, they were created in His image, which would have been sinless perfection, knowing only how to do good and to please God. Everything that He created for them in the Garden of Eden was all for their use, but with one exception; God forbade them to eat the fruit of the tree of the knowledge of good and evil, because He knew that if they ate of it, they would suddenly become aware of how to do things that are sinful and evil.

But they were tempted by Satan to disobey God's command, and so they ate this forbidden fruit. At that moment their eyes were opened, and they realised what they had done. Because of their rebellion, God banished them from the Garden of Eden and posted angels at its gates to prevent them from ever entering it again. All humanity, since The Fall of Adam and Eve, has been born with the inherent disposition of that **original sin of rebellion against God's Word**. It is hardwired into our DNA.

As a consequence of The Fall, the default position of every human being is that we will spend eternity in hell because of our inherent sinful state. We all stand outside the 'Garden' (heaven) and something needs to happen to enable us to be made right with God so that we may enter in. We all need to be saved in order to receive eternal life in God's kingdom. Salvation has only been made available to us through Jesus Christ:

"And there is salvation in no one else; for there is ***no other name*** *under heaven that has been given among people* ***by which we must be saved*** *[for God has provided the world no alternative for salvation]."* – Acts 4:12 AMP (Authors' emphasis)

There is No Alternative

There is **no alternative**, despite the multitude of bogus and deceptive claims of other spiritual organisations offering a spiritual path to salvation and eternal life by a means **other** than through faith in Jesus Christ. Such claims are an attempt to get into heaven through the wrong gate. The only gate to eternal life is through the narrow gate of faith in Jesus Christ and what He has accomplished on the cross for our salvation. Every other gate that is on offer by the world is a counterfeit, leading all who choose to go through those gates to end up in hell. Without faith in Jesus Christ **alone**, we will not be permitted entry into heaven. When we come to draw our last breath, if we have failed to believe and trust in Jesus for our eternal salvation, we will weep in much sorrow. Putting our trust in the lies created by the alternative spiritual organisations of this world, which are dressed up to look like the truth, will not save us. Even if we are not following the teachings of other spiritual organisations but are simply living the best we can as 'good people', our good works on their own will not save us or get us into heaven. Millions of people who do not have any kind of faith still think or hope that they will get into heaven or go to a 'better place' when they die, but the Word of God confirms that salvation is only through faith in Jesus Christ (see the Scripture above and the ones ahead).

Fire! Fire!

If your house was on fire and someone showed you that there was **only one way** to escape and save your life, why would you refuse to follow that person to safety? Why would you choose to remain in the fire trying to find another way to save yourself, risking being burned alive in the flames? No one likes to think about hell, but it is a scriptural reality. Jesus spoke about hell many times. Peter stood up and told us what we need to do to be saved, and why (see Acts Chapter 2). God's way of salvation through faith in Jesus Christ is the only way of escape from the raging fires of hell.

Claiming to Know God

Many people claim to know God, but that is as far as their belief in Him goes, yet they seem to believe that all will be well for their soul when they die. The Bible says that we must believe in the only way of salvation that God has provided, and nothing else. God's Word teaches us that we must repent of our sin, put our faith in Jesus Christ and live godly lives in obedience to His Word. When we reject God's Word, yet still profess to 'know God', we may find ourselves on the wrong side of the gate when the time comes for our soul to leave our body at our death.

"Not everyone who says to me, 'Lord, Lord,' will enter the kingdom of heaven, but only the one who does the will of my Father who is in heaven." – Matthew 7:21 NIV

How do we know whether we 'know God', and what is the 'will of the Father'? The passage below gives us the answer:

"And we can be sure that we know him if we obey his commandments. If someone claims, "I know God," but doesn't obey

God's commandments, that person is a liar and is not living in the truth. But those who obey God's word truly show how completely they love him. *That is how we know we are living in him. Those who say they live in God should live their lives as Jesus did."* – 1 John 2:3-6 (Authors' emphasis)

The Amplified Bible puts that passage in a very powerful way, which should leave us without any doubt as to who truly are followers of Christ, and who are the ones who simply say they 'know God', but do not obey His Word.

"And this is how we know [daily, by experience] that we have come to know Him [to understand Him and be more deeply acquainted with Him]: if we habitually keep [focused on His precepts and obey] His commandments (teachings). Whoever says, "I have come to know Him," but does not habitually keep [focused on His precepts and obey] His commandments (teachings), is a liar, and the truth [of the divine word] is not in him. ***But whoever habitually keeps His word and obeys His precepts [and treasures His message in its entirety]****, in him the love of God has truly been perfected [it is completed and has reached maturity]. By this we know [for certain] that we are in Him: whoever says he lives in Christ [that is, whoever says he has accepted Him as God and Savior] ought [as a moral obligation] to walk and conduct himself just as He walked and conducted Himself."* – 1 John 2:3-6 AMP (Authors' emphasis)

From this passage we can conclude that those who say they know God but do not obey His Word, are liars and are not followers of Christ at all, despite however much they may profess to be. It is obedience to God's Word that is the benchmark that reveals if someone is a true follower of Christ, or not. If we say that we know God, but do not obey His Word, (i.e. we do not solely believe that His Word is the only authority on salvation, and we pick and mix His Word with a host of other teachings from other spiritual belief systems), may this revelation from the above Scripture passage convict us to do all that is necessary to put the matter right, as a matter of urgency.

Take Action... Now!

Finally, if you know that you are not a follower of Christ and want to be sure of your salvation and entering into heaven when you die, we urge you to take action now! Get on your knees and cry out to God to save you. Admit and confess to Him that you are a sinner in need of salvation, and that you want to repent of your sins. Tell Him that you realise that what Jesus endured on the cross for you is your only hope of salvation, and that you now put your faith in His amazing sacrifice of love, mercy, grace and forgiveness which has been provided for you through His broken body and His shed blood. Tell God that you want to live your life in faith in Jesus, and to obey His Word. Ask God to fill you with the Holy Spirit so that He can begin to work in you to transform your life and enable you to live a godly life. Find a Bible-believing church that upholds the Scriptures and refuses to compromise with it. It may take some time to find such a church in the times in which we now live, but pray to God to lead you to one that is faithful to His Word.

Not a day can be wasted in the uncertainty of wondering where your soul will go when your mortal body dies. You need to know for certain **now**; it will be too late when your soul leaves your body. If you want to be certain of being saved and dwelling in heaven for eternity, then the only way to be sure of this is to put your faith in Jesus Christ and to ask Him to be your Lord and Saviour.

Now that you have finished reading this book, we would like to encourage you to fall on your knees and make this action the very next thing that you do. Your eternal destiny depends upon it.

Notes

Chapter 1

1. Hill, Clifford, *The Reshaping of Britain - Church and State since the 1960s: A Personal Reflection*, (London: Wilberforce Publications, 2018) p. 12. Used by permission.

2. Taken from the morning reading dated 13th June of *Daily Readings from All Four Gospels: For Morning and Evening* by J.C. Ryle.
   EP BOOKS, 1st Floor Venture House, 6 Silver Court, Watchmead, Welwyn Garden City, UK, AL7 1TS
   Used by permission. www.epbooks.org

3. Taken from the morning reading dated 23rd June of *Daily Readings from All Four Gospels: For Morning and Evening* by J.C. Ryle.
   EP BOOKS, 1st Floor Venture House, 6 Silver Court, Watchmead, Welwyn Garden City, UK, AL7 1TS
   Used by permission. www.epbooks.org

Chapter 2

1. Taken from the evening reading dated 4th May of *Daily Readings from All Four Gospels: For Morning and Evening* by J.C. Ryle.
   EP BOOKS, 1st Floor Venture House, 6 Silver Court, Watchmead, Welwyn Garden City, UK, AL7 1TS
   Used by permission. www.epbooks.org

2. Taken from the evening reading dated 4th June of *Daily Readings from All Four Gospels: For Morning and Evening* by J.C. Ryle.
   EP BOOKS, 1st Floor Venture House, 6 Silver Court, Watchmead, Welwyn Garden City, UK, AL7 1TS
   Used by permission. www.epbooks.org

3. Franks, Nicholas Paul, *BODY ZERO – Radical Preparation for the Return of Christ* p.30. Used by permission.

4. Hill, Clifford, *The Reshaping of Britain - Church and State since the 1960s: A Personal Reflection*, (London: Wilberforce Publications, 2018) p. 32-33. Used by permission.

5. A quote by Andrea Williams; Founder of *Christian Concern*, 70 Wimpole Street, London W1G 8AX. Used by permission. www.christianconcern.com

Chapter 3

1. Taken from the evening reading dated 4th May of *Daily Readings from All Four Gospels: For Morning and Evening* by J.C. Ryle.
   EP BOOKS, 1st Floor Venture House, 6 Silver Court, Watchmead, Welwyn Garden City, UK, AL7 1TS
   Used by permission. www.epbooks.org

2. Ryle, J.C. *Warnings to the Churches*: p. 44. The Banner of Truth Trust, 3 Murrayfield Road, Edinburgh, EH12 6EL, UK. Used by permission. www.banneroftruth.org

Chapter 4

1. Taken from the morning reading dated 1st July of *Daily Readings from All Four Gospels: For Morning and Evening* by J.C. Ryle.
   EP BOOKS, 1st Floor Venture House, 6 Silver Court, Watchmead, Welwyn Garden City, UK, AL7 1TS
   Used by permission. www.epbooks.org

2. The words of The Reverend John Parker quoted to *Christian Concern*, 70 Wimpole Street, London W1G 8AX. Used by permission. www.christianconcern.com

3. Hill, Clifford, *The Reshaping of Britain - Church and State since the 1960s: A Personal Reflection*, (London: Wilberforce Publications, 2018) p. 104. Used by permission.

4. Hill, Clifford, *The Reshaping of Britain - Church and State since the 1960s: A Personal Reflection*, (London: Wilberforce Publications, 2018) p. 53. Used by permission.

5. Hill, Clifford, *The Reshaping of Britain - Church and State since the 1960s: A Personal Reflection*, (London: Wilberforce Publications, 2018) p. 305. Used by permission.

6. www.onebodyonefaith.org.uk

7. www.billygraham.org

8. Hill, Clifford, *The Reshaping of Britain - Church and State since the 1960s: A Personal Reflection*, (London: Wilberforce Publications, 2018) p. 21. Used by permission.

9. Hill, Clifford, *The Reshaping of Britain - Church and State since the 1960s: A Personal Reflection*, (London: Wilberforce Publications, 2018) p. 79. Used by permission.

10. A quote by The Right Reverend Dr Gavin Ashenden. Used by permission.

11. A quote by Andrea Williams; Founder of *Christian Concern*, 70 Wimpole Street, London W1G 8AX. Used by permission. www.christianconcern.com

Chapter 5

1. Ryle, J.C. *REPENTANCE – Its Nature, Necessity and Encouragement*: Taken from page 27-28 (Icthus Press, Scotland, UK.)

2. Taken from the morning reading dated 7th May of *Daily Readings from All Four Gospels: For Morning and Evening* by J.C. Ryle.
   EP BOOKS, 1st Floor Venture House, 6 Silver Court, Watchmead, Welwyn Garden City, UK, AL7 1TS
   Used by permission. www.epbooks.org

Epilogue

1. Tsarfati Amir, *The Last Hour – An Israeli Insider Looks at the End Times*. p. 175-176. (Chosen Books, 11400 Hampshire Avenue South, Bloomington, Minnesota 55438). Used by permission. www.bakerpublishinggroup.com

2. Hill, Clifford, *The Reshaping of Britain - Church and State since the 1960s: A Personal Reflection*, (London: Wilberforce Publications, 2018) p. 13-14. Used by permission.

3. Ryle, J.C. *Are You Ready For The End Of Time? Understanding Future Events from Prophetic Passages of the Bible*: p. 38.
   Christian Focus Publications Ltd, Geanies House, Fearn, Tain, Ross–shire IV20 1TW, Scotland, UK.
   Used by permission. www.christianfocus.com

Recommended Reading

1. Carter, J.W. *Trumpet Blast Warning*
   ISBN: 9780992795207

2. Ryle, J.C. *Are You Ready for the End of Time? Understanding Future Events from Prophetic Passages of the Bible*
   ISBN: 1857927478.

3. Ryle, J.C. *Warnings to the Churches*
   ISBN: 9780851510439

4. Ryle, J.C. *Separation from the World*
   ISBN-13: 9781611045499

5. Ryle, J.C. *REPENTANCE*
   ISBN: 9781535339230

6. Ryle, J.C. *Heading for Heaven*
   ISBN-13: 9780852347102

7. Hill, Clifford, *The Reshaping of Britain – Church and State since the 1960s: A Personal Reflection*
   ISBN: 9780995683297

8. Tsarfati Amir, *The Last Hour – An Israeli Insider Looks at the End Times*
   ISBN: 978-0-8007-9912-0

9. Franks, Nicholas Paul, *BODY ZERO – Radical Preparation for the Return of Christ*
   ISBN: 978-1-78815-714-8

10. Bloomer, George, *Witchcraft in the Pews*
    ISBN: 9781629118581

11. Various contributors, *The New Normal – The Transgender Agenda*
    ISBN: 9780995683259

About the Authors

Chris and Michele Neal live in the United Kingdom, and have been born again, Spirit-filled Christians since the early 1990's. The burden that they both carry in their hearts is to wake up followers of Christ from the slumber that has come upon the Church in the times that we now live. Chris' passion is in the area of Men's Ministry, to disciple men into right and godly living, in obedience to God's Holy Word. Michele's calling is in the area of the Church as a whole, to wake it up to what Jesus has to say about sin **within** the Church, about the End Times, and false gospels that are spreading like wildfire, not only in the modern Church, but now also affecting the established, traditional Church; an institution which once held steadfast to the truth of God's Word in the face of whatever came against it.

In between writing books, Chris is a semi-retired sales and marketing professional, and Michele is a housewife. For rest and relaxation, they enjoy time out by the sea and visiting tea shops.

The Authors' other Books

Chris' Book – Available on Amazon

The Christian Book for Men – Biblical Solutions to the Battles Facing Men

Paperback: ISBN 9781794347212

Kindle: ASIN B07ND42SRY

Visit Chris' website
www.thechristianbookformen.com

Michele's Books – Available on Amazon

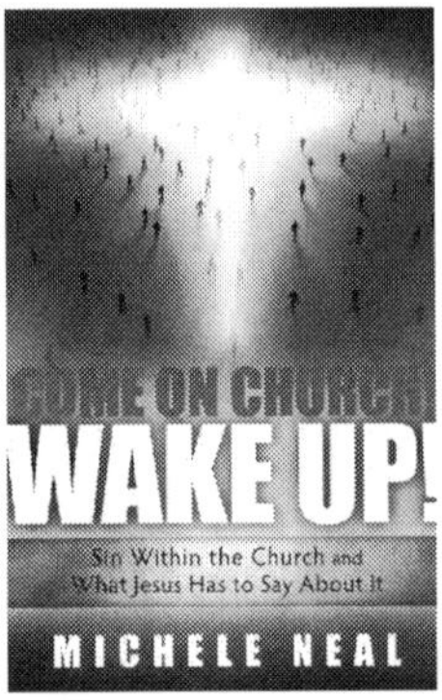

Come on Church! Wake Up! – Sin Within the Church and What Jesus Has to Say About It

Paperback: ISBN 978-1-62136-316-3

Kindle: ISBN 978-1-62136-315-6

The End of The World and What Jesus Has to Say About It

Paperback: ISBN 978-1-62136-742-0

Kindle: ISBN 978-1-62136-743-7

The Gospel of Deception – Counterfeit Christianity and the Fate of Its Followers

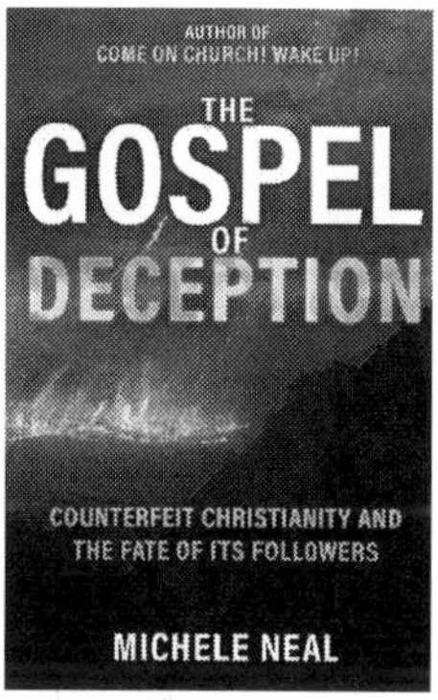

Paperback: ISBN 978-1974387014
Kindle: ISBN 1974387011

When Healing Doesn't Happen – A Life Lived for God through the Journey of Suffering

Paperback: ISBN: 978-1099706455
Kindle: ISBN: 1099706459

Visit Michele's website
www.michelenealuk.com

Printed in Great Britain
by Amazon

48450704R00129